Praise for the Power of the Learning Mindset

"Developing a learning mindset as a leader is one of the most important qualities you can build. Lilian and Marshall are two of the best in the world, and this book is a masterclass—essential reading for all leaders!"

—Alisa Cohn, executive coach and author of
From Start-Up to Grown-Up

"Great leadership begins with a willingness to learn, intentional choices about how to grow, and the nurturing of others' potential. In *The Power of the Learning Mindset*, Lillian Ajayi Ore and Marshall Goldsmith bring these timeless truths to life in a way that is practical, inspiring, and deeply human."

—Dr. Raghu Krishnamoorthy, senior fellow
and director, Penn's Chief Learning Officer
Executive Doctoral Program, and former CHRO, GE

"*The Power of the Learning Mindset* is an inspiring guide for anyone determined to lead with curiosity, adaptability, and vision. Lilian Ajayi Ore and Marshall Goldsmith show that true leadership is not about having all the answers but about cultivating the discipline to keep learning and helping others grow. This book is a powerful resource for professionals ready to thrive in a world of constant change."

—Troy J. Eggers, dean, School of Professional Studies,
Columbia University

"In *The Power of the Learning Mindset*, Lilian Ajayi Ore and Marshall Goldsmith illuminate something essential: in a world defined by exponentializing change and uncertainty, it's not a leader's credentials or past wins that determine their future—it's their capacity to learn, adapt, and grow. Goldsmith's hallmark clarity in leadership coaching paired with Ore's deep expertise in organizational growth gives this book an unusually powerful combination of inspiration, groundedness, and practicality.

From developing emotional intelligence and fostering curiosity to distinguishing lasting value from trends—each chapter equips leaders with tools and strategies to cultivate learning cultures that don't just survive disruption but thrive in it. What sets this book apart is its ability to translate profound concepts, research-proven pedagogical techniques, and motivational theories into new practical strategies that can be applied immediately in individual and organizational contexts. Full of rigor, insight, and rooted in decades of research and real-time leadership experience, this book doesn't simply tell you why a learning mindset matters—it shows you how to make it the foundation of your work, teams, and life. For anyone serious about leading with purpose and thriving through change, this book is an indispensable guide and a North Star."

—**Dr. Sharon Ravitch PhD, professor of practice, University of Pennsylvania**

"This book is a timely reminder that learning isn't just an individual pursuit; it's a leadership imperative. When you embrace curiosity, ambition, and a growth mindset, you can inspire others and create lasting impact."

—**Lucy Swedberg, editor, *Higher Education***

"A powerful call to lead through learning! *The Power of the Learning Mindset* is an inspiring and practical guide for leaders at every level. Dr. Ajayi Ore and Dr. Goldsmith show how a commitment to continuous learning unlocks personal growth, drives innovation, and transforms organizational culture. With real-world examples, actionable strategies, and a focus on purpose-driven leadership, this book empowers readers to take ownership of their development—and lead with impact."

—Julie Carrier, global authority on leadership development for young people, Thinkers50 Ideas into Practice Award Winner, and founder, The Leadership Development Institute for Young Women

"*The Power of the Learning Mindset* is an essential masterclass for today's leaders. Dr. Lilian Ajayi Ore and Marshall Goldsmith reveal what it truly takes to *win* in an ever-evolving, post-pandemic workplace. This powerful book is a must-read for executives who aspire to elevate their leadership, empower their teams, and achieve lasting growth."

—HRH, Chief Temitope Ajayi, chairman and CEO, SV-NED Inc.

THE POWER OF THE LEARNING MINDSET

LILIAN AJAYI ORE

MARSHALL GOLDSMITH

Foreword by ERIC SCHURENBERG

THE POWER OF THE LEARNING MINDSET

How the Best Leaders *Foster Curiosity,*
Develop Innovative Teams, and
Achieve Exponential Growth

WILEY

Published by John Wiley & Sons, Inc., Hoboken, New Jersey.

For general information on our other products and services or for technical support, please contact our Customer Care Department within the United States at (800) 762-2974, outside the United States at (317) 572-3993 or fax (317) 572-4002.

Wiley also publishes its books in a variety of electronic formats. Some content that appears in print may not be available in electronic formats. For more information about Wiley products, visit our web site at www.wiley.com.

Library of Congress Cataloging-in-Publication Data is Available:

ISBN 9781394324569 (Cloth)
ISBN 9781394324576 (ePub)
ISBN 9781394324583 (ePDF)

Cover Design: Jon Boylan
Cover Image: © Sylverarts/stock.adobe.com
Author Photos: © Oluwaseye Olusa, © Dr. Marshall Goldsmith

Printed and bound by CPI Group (UK) Ltd, Croydon, CR0 4YY

C9781394324569_140126

Here's to the courageous leader in you—curious, aspirational, and committed to excellence in both practice and purpose.

Contents

Foreword

Eric Schurenberg

In my role as the founder of the Alliance for Trust in Media, I try to help people discern what is true. In the chaos of a 21st-century news feed, the answer is rarely obvious. I often get the exasperated question, "Can't you just tell me who (which newspaper, commentator, podcaster, cable TV network, influencer) is telling the truth?" If only it were that easy.

In the Introduction to this inspiring book, Dr. Lilian refers to social influence theory, or confirmation bias: the hard-wired tendency to believe evidence that supports your beliefs and to discard any that contradicts them. The more validation an information source offers, the more credible it seems. The bias applies not just to us consumers of information but also to the people who share it. That's not necessarily gullibility on our part or dishonesty on theirs. It's simply being human.

What I tell people is not to place their belief in any particular authority, but instead to look for a process. And on finding it, trust that. You can call that process the scientific method, or jurisprudence, or journalistic integrity, or intellectual humility—or, as Dr. Lilian does, *learning prowess*. It's intentional open-mindedness, a willingness to admit evidence that challenges your beliefs, and above all, a commitment to consider no proposition to be above reasonable challenge. In deciding who to trust, the all-too-human tendency is to trust those who are the cleverest at defending what you already believe. My advice, and Dr. Lilian's, would be to look instead for evidence of learning prowess in your source of information. That will expose you sometimes to evidence you'd rather ignore. But that's a feature, not a bug.

I think about how useful Dr. Lilian's *The Power of the Learning Mindset* would have been to me when I was the CEO of Inc. and Fast Company. One of the signature tasks of leadership is to understand what is really happening in your organization—even if the truth is unpleasant—and to foster a dedication to truth in your colleagues. Their tendency will be to figure out what you want to hear and deliver only that. This is normal. A learning mindset, however, requires you to resist it.

Dr. Lilian brings the lens of an educator to this book, a commitment both to intellectual humility and to the rigorous pursuit of knowledge. Her coauthor, Marshall Goldsmith, brings the wisdom of decades spent advising the world's most accomplished leaders, reminding them that the skills that carried them to the top may not be the ones that will sustain them there. Together, they make a compelling case for the learning mindset as an essential quality for leadership.

Essential, yes, but you shouldn't imagine that the learning mindset is something you can achieve and be done with, a box to check off. Instead, it's something to aspire to—a journey of progress without a finish line. As a teacher of media literacy, for example, I still find myself doing constant battle against my own confirmation bias. As a business leader, I continually had to resist the comfortable urge to accept business problems as permanently solved and beliefs (about the markets, emerging technologies, competitors, and so on) as settled knowledge.

The beauty of this book is that it lays out the milestones along the journey that is the learning mindset. The initial gating factor is willingness: the discipline to put curiosity and intellectual humility above the urge to be "right." Willingness unlocks the ability to apply intention to your interactions with your team and to nurture a culture of learning in yourself and your organization.

I'd encourage you to read on, then, with an open mind. Absorb the lessons and examples in the book, and you'll shift how you see the information flowing through your company—and your life. You'll see more broadly and more clearly. You'll end up believing, as I do, that in the near-constant disruptions of the 21st century, a commitment to learning may be the closest thing any company can have to a durable advantage.

"No one is ever above learning"
>> —Teyana Taylor, American singer-songwriter,
>> actress, and choreographer

Introduction: The Rise, Fall, and Rebirth of the Learning Prowess

Has Truth Lost Its Relevance?

In today's world, we are overwhelmed by the distractions of misinformation, disinformation, clickbait headlines, declining institutional trust, and self-proclaimed experts. Not to mention the allure of celebrity gossip, the endless scroll of social media opinions from friends and strangers alike, political noise, digital scams, and the lingering effects of post-pandemic fatigue.

Americans now spend an average of 21 hours per week streaming content—a trend mirrored around the globe—while daily social media use continues to climb. These digital habits often pull us away from meaningful relationships, personal growth, and the pursuit of healthier routines.

We are in the midst of a personal time crisis—one that's reshaping how we relate to truth itself. As the boundaries between reality and illusion swing like a pendulum, the very idea of truth becomes blurred, leaving us to question not just what is true but also whether truth still matters at all.

Are we also losing our ability to distinguish fact from fiction? In the midst of this information overload, our mental models are shifting. We may find ourselves clinging to familiar "truths" simply because they feel recognizable—even if they no longer serve us.

At the same time, we often absorb what's presented to us without urgency, curiosity, or critical examination. In this environment, convenience can replace credibility, and familiarity can override fact.

This phenomenon surprisingly isn't new. Sociologists have long discussed *social influence theory*, which explains the human tendency to seek conformity and social proof from loved ones, peers, and society at large—especially when our social ties influence our perceptions of reality.

This need for validation often stops us from exploring deeper truths and instead leaves us settling for surface-level narratives, keeps us busy, and swayed by a disappearing reverence for the unvarnished truth.

Eric Schurenberg, founder of the Alliance for Trust in Media and former editor-in-chief of *Fast Company* and *Inc. Magazine* —a friend, mentor, and fellow member of the Marshall Goldsmith 100 Coaches—captured this dilemma during a classroom discussion.

Eric shares, "we are witnessing the erosion of truth-telling and its effect on everyone. This is the time to invest in our mental immunity. Get outside your bubble to get a different perspective. Don't imagine that you, or your group, have a monopoly on truth."

Eric, a distinguished business journalist and media executive, leads an organization at the forefront of the fight against misinformation and disinformation—working to restore trust in professional journalism and protect our shared understanding of truth in a rapidly changing media landscape.

Society's continued acceptance of others' interpretations of truth underscores why the subtitle to this Introduction is titled, "The Rise, Fall, and Rebirth of the Learning Prowess."

Prowess represents the relentless pursuit of knowledge and the drive to live out our aspirations. It is a personal journey and a commitment to self-betterment, creating value not only for ourselves but also for others.

Prowess embodies the desire to learn, reskill, and show up differently in a world rife with distraction and noise. Prowess is often mistaken for mastery, but is there a difference between the two? We say yes.

Mastery is often viewed as a fixed destination—a state of complete skill and expertise in a specific area, suggesting an endpoint achieved through consistent effort and control.

Prowess, however, extends beyond mastery; it is a continuous journey toward excellence, truth, and adaptability. Unlike mastery, which implies a final achievement, prowess emphasizes resilience, authenticity, and the ongoing refinement of skills and knowledge. It is a commitment to lifelong learning.

It's an evolving commitment to growth, challenging individuals to constantly expand their potential and integrate new insights. This perspective on prowess is essential for organizations seeking to cultivate a talent pool that values continuous growth over static achievement.

By fostering a culture where the power of the learning mindsets is prioritized, organizations can develop teams that are adaptable, curious, innovative, and driven to excel beyond mere mastery. However, research reveals a concerning trend: many organizations today struggle to build a workplace culture that genuinely rewards the pursuit of prowess over static achievement or, at times, disengagement.

Leadership's Role in Creating a Culture of Prowess

Ultimately, creating an environment that prioritizes prowess lies with leadership. Leaders set the tone and serve as role models, amplifying the importance of continuous growth and signaling to employees that learning, adaptability, and innovation are highly valued.

By actively engaging in their own development and encouraging a shared commitment to learning, leaders can inspire a culture where prowess is celebrated over mere compliance.

To amplify the need for prowess, leaders must do more than encourage learning; they must cultivate a growth-oriented mindset at all levels. This means recognizing and rewarding progress, promoting open-mindedness, and providing opportunities for employees to pursue challenging, meaningful work that fosters ongoing skill refinement.

Leaders should also create safe spaces for experimentation, where employees feel empowered to take risks and explore new ideas without fear of failure or judgment.

Addressing the challenge of cultivating prowess-oriented cultures is crucial for strengthening a collective commitment to growth and fostering an environment where knowledge, innovation, and meaningful success can thrive.

This book is dedicated to supporting leaders and organizations on their journey back to prowess—reclaiming the paradox of truth for seekers and lifelong learners alike.

By prioritizing intentional learning, curiosity, and the development of a growth-oriented mindset, we can create environments where thoughtfulness, innovation, and authentic growth are not only encouraged but thrive.

Leaders who champion prowess inspire their teams to think critically, challenge assumptions, and pursue excellence—not as a static achievement but as an ongoing, dynamic process.

Together, we can strengthen the foundations of leadership and learning, building a future where organizations and individuals alike are empowered to grow, adapt, and lead with integrity.

Leading with the WIN Mindset

In a world where everyone wants to win and avoid losing, we're often told that success is reserved for the privileged or the exceptionally courageous. But Marshall and I believe winning isn't just for the select few—it's a mindset shift accessible to all.

Winning is about adopting a mindset that empowers us to take control of our growth, confront our fears, and shape our futures.

Take Tony Robbins, bestselling author and renowned performance coach, for example. In high school, he began to realize the power of what we call the WIN mindset—a shift in thinking that transformed his reality.

Tony frequently wondered why his family struggled financially while others could afford luxury vacations and enjoy stability. His determination to reshape his future led him to adopt a mindset focused on change, monetary success, social impact, and achievement.

By concentrating on what he could accomplish, Robbins moved from modest beginnings to becoming a multimillionaire, demonstrating that mindset is a powerful driver of success.

Our WIN mindset model, with its foundation in Willingness, Intentionality, and Nurturing, is accessible to everyone who's ready to make a change. It's not merely about achieving goals but about nurturing a mindset that fuels growth, resilience, and sustained progress.

A Quest for Prowess: Learning, Leadership, and Coaching

The purpose of this book is to support leaders and aspiring leaders in shaping their professional legacy, amplifying thought leadership, and achieving both career and life aspirations. Through personal anecdotes and real-life examples, we will share how our commitment to learning prowess transformed our leadership and coaching abilities. The WIN mindset model of willingness, intentionality, and nurturing will guide you through your next leadership transformation journey.

The WIN mindset model will serve as your road map to mastering learning, leadership, and coaching prowess while helping you achieve your goals and aspirations and uplifting your team and supporting their prowess. Through practical advice, actionable strategies, and reflective exercises, you'll be equipped to apply these principles daily, enhancing your ability to lead, inspire, and drive positive change.

By picking up this book, you've already committed to shaping your learning prowess and developing the ability to learn faster, lead better, and inspire transformation in yourself, your team, and the world around you.

Like you, Marshall and I have sought answers and professional growth through a journey of learning. This quest transformed us into the leaders we are today, and in this book, we will share what sparked our learning prowess and how it shaped our individual paths. The WIN mindset model is integrated throughout the book's three core concepts: learning prowess, leadership prowess, and coaching prowess as seen in Figure 1a.

Each of the book's three parts reflects an essential aspect of the WIN mindset model. Part 1, "The Learning Prowess," focuses on the willingness to learn, fostering an open mindset ready for growth and continuous development. Part 2, "Developing Leadership Prowess," focuses on intentionality—leading with

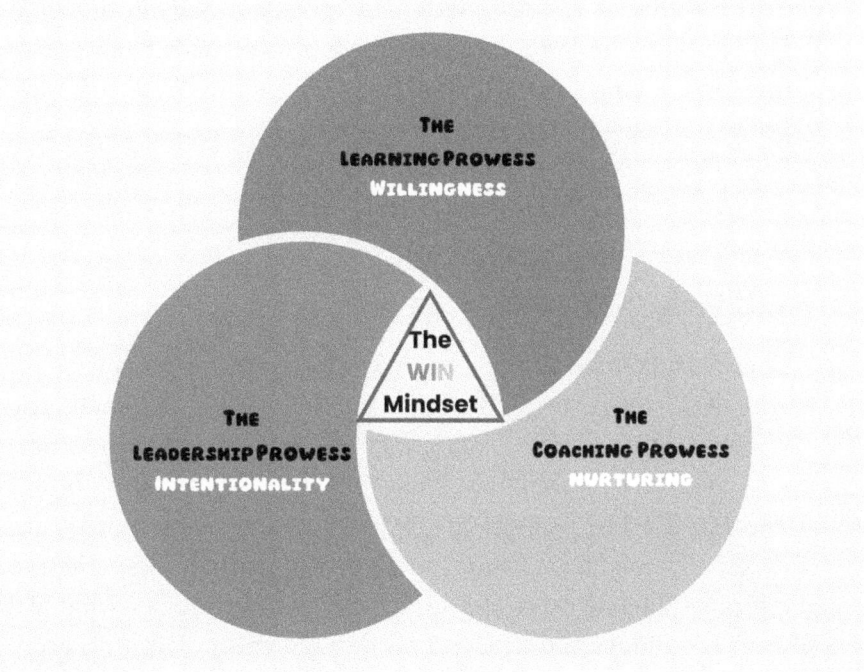

FIGURE 1a The WIN mindset model.

intention, purpose, and clarity of direction. Part 3, "Embracing Coaching Prowess," emphasizes on nurturing, inspiring growth by supporting and developing others.

The Role of Truth in the WIN Mindset

The WIN mindset integrates truth as a vital element in learning, leadership, and coaching prowess. Willingness requires the courage to confront truths about oneself and embrace the need for growth. Intentionality calls for acting with purpose based on truth, ensuring decisions are grounded in reality. Nurturing fosters environments where truth can be shared openly, building trust, and promoting genuine development.

Truth acts as the foundation for personal and professional growth, and the WIN mindset offers a clear path to integrate this into your pursuit of learning, leadership, and coaching prowess, a new level to self-leadership.

Aligning Leadership with Self-Improvement

There needs to be a much stronger alignment between leaders and their desire for self-improvement, which Marshall, the world's number one executive coach, and my coauthor, describes in his latest *The New York Times*–bestselling book, *The Earned Life*, as the triple A model. The triple As are expressed as action, ambition, and aspiration—where *action* refers to what we are doing now, *ambition* reflects what we want to achieve, and *aspiration* defines whom we ultimately want to become.

Marshall's observations from working with top executives reveal that how an executive approaches each of these three elements determines the level of their career success.

Action alone tends to be short-sighted because actions are often aimed at immediate gratification. Whether it's dietary decisions, exercise routines, or on-the-job decision-making, actions are passive or active but can often lack long-term consequences or alignment with a larger vision.

Ambition is more focused—it drives us toward a specific outcome or milestone, typically time-bound. For example, an executive might think, "I will complete the leadership program, apply the knowledge to my team, or hit a sales target to get a promotion." While this is a strong motivator for many successful people, it is still goal-oriented and finite.

Aspiration, however, transcends short-term outcomes and is not constrained by a finish line. Aspiration reflects a deeper sense of purpose and continuous growth. As Marshall eloquently states in the book, *Earned Life*, "Our aspirations may change over time, but they don't go away, whether we articulate them or not. We stop aspiring when we stop breathing."

But is one better than the other? Marshall argues that when the triple As are combined and interdependent, executives become unstoppable, and fulfillment becomes a reality. This isn't true just for executives. It's true for all leaders.

Bringing It Together: The WIN Mindset and the Triple A Model

Willingness connects with *action*. Leaders must be willing to take immediate actions, to reflect on where they are now, and be open to growth. Willingness is the first step in aligning with one's future path.

Intentionality aligns with *ambition*. Intentionality, like ambition, requires focus and purpose. It directs leaders toward achieving specific outcomes while remaining aligned with their core values and leadership goals.

Nurturing integrates with *aspiration*. Nurturing long-term growth and supporting others in their leadership and coaching journeys reflects a broader, more profound aspiration. This is not about achieving a single goal but about continuous evolution and legacy building.

Marshall's triple A model perfectly complements the WIN mindset, demonstrating that a balance between immediate actions, goal-driven ambitions, and lifelong aspirations can unlock a leader's true potential and lead to not just success but also fulfillment.

The Path to Trusted Leadership and Legacy

With a comprehensive approach to trusted leadership and legacy, we hope this book empowers you with the mindsets and skills needed to achieve your next WIN—whether that means shaping your professional legacy, amplifying your thought leadership, building innovative teams, or driving meaningful business outcomes. More important, this book is designed to help you forge clear pathways toward fulfilling both your career ambitions and life aspirations.

A key part of this journey is becoming a more effective trusted advisor. Today's leaders are being called—by their teams, their cultures, and society at large—to show up with greater trust, insight, and integrity.

Dr. Keith Keating, award-winning author and friend, defines a *trusted learning advisor* as "someone respected for their knowledge and guidance, who provides advice, perspective, and information."

This book champions the development of leaders who want to elevate their learning, leadership, and coaching prowess—an essential formula for decisive leadership and long-term success in today's complex world.

Becoming a trusted advisor is not optional—it is critical to recruiting, retaining, and sustaining organizational excellence.

Through this book, you will learn how to do the following:

- Strengthen your learning, leadership, and coaching skills to enable decisive leadership.
- Cultivate a growth-oriented mindset aligned with both short and long-term goals.
- Become a trusted advisor who inspires and drives organizational success.
- Lead with purpose, intention, clarity, and accountability.

- Build cultures rooted in trust, credibility, and continuous learning.
- Create a lasting legacy by passing on knowledge and values to future leaders.

Our sincere hope is that you finish this book with a renewed sense of purpose, greater leadership intention, and a deeper commitment to social responsibility and personal accountability.

Ultimately, the power of this book lies in your decision to embrace the WIN mindset—your internal compass for progress, growth, and sustained excellence across every dimension of life.

The WIN mindset is the key to unlocking your true learning, leadership, and coaching prowess. Through practical guidance and reflective exercises, you'll enhance your ability to learn faster, lead with impact, and spark meaningful transformation in yourself and others.

The pursuit of prowess is not a moment—it's a lifelong mission. This book is your road map.

1

The Quest for Prowess

Why Everyone Needs a Prowess Map

The quest for prowess is likely the reason you've chosen to pick up this book.

In this chapter, you'll uncover the moment and event that drives the desire to seek and expand one's prowess—a pivotal experience that propels you to learn more and to continue learning. For some, this quest emerges from a singular incident; for others, it's a gradual realization.

For me, this journey was shaped by a sequence of events that transformed my life. Unlike mastery, prowess is a lifestyle—a commitment fueled by passion, drive, and purpose, grounded in a clear understanding of what's required to create meaningful outcomes and alternative realities.

This pivotal moment is illustrated in Figure 1.1. In the sections that follow, we'll explore the intricacies of the prowess map and explain why everyone needs one as a tool for intentional growth and leadership clarity.

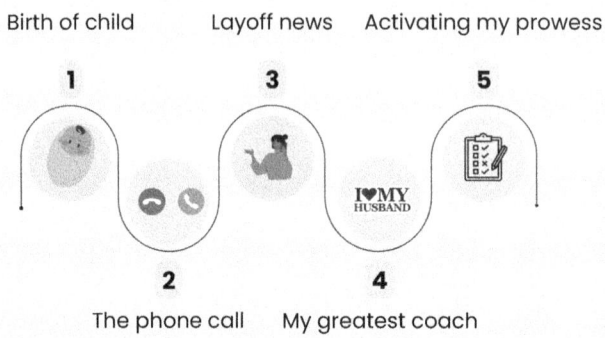

Birth of child   Layoff news   Activating my prowess

1   3   5

2   4

The phone call   My greatest coach

FIGURE 1.1 My prowess map.

Unpacking the Map: A Life-Altering Moment

It was Sunday, September 18, 2016. I was overwhelmed with joy, lying in my hospital bed and gazing at my first child, who was peacefully asleep beside me. It was one of the happiest days of my life.

Only three hours had passed since I had given birth, and as my newborn son and I rested, my phone rang with an unexpected call. I answered, unconcerned about the timing, only to hear unexpected news that I was being laid off.

As the caller went on, I found myself tuning out. It's common to disconnect after hearing the words, "You're being laid off." I froze—numb and confused. The emotional high from my recent delivery had overpowered my ability to fully process the disappointment and fear that came with losing my job.

When the call ended abruptly, leaving me with a mix of emotions—joy for my newborn and the jarring shock of job loss. I wondered silently how I would manage without the stability of a full-time income.

A New Perspective: From Loss to Purpose

When my husband, Alexander, returned to the hospital with extra clothes for me, I waited to share the news. As he stared at his son in his crib, with pride and joy, I hesitated, not wanting to taint the moment with my layoff news.

But eventually, I shared it.

His response would forever solidify his role as my greatest coach and accountability partner: "Now you can focus on your passion for teaching," he said.

Alexander—a natural leader and top executive—had an effortless way of inspiring and managing people. Though his response initially shocked me, his unwavering support and vision were qualities I had always admired in him.

A Journey Rooted in Teaching and Impact

By this point in my career, I have been teaching as an adjunct professor and guest lecturer at various higher education institutions both in the United States and abroad.

Teaching is my passion. I thrived in the classroom, energized by the opportunity to work closely with students, share insights, and make a meaningful impact in their careers.

As a practitioner, I brought a real-world perspective to my students, offering them insights into business challenges and workplace dynamics. Their curiosity fueled my passion, and I was deeply committed to helping them shape their career aspirations. My classes filled quickly, and many students reached out, hoping to move from the waitlist into the classroom.

Investing in Prowess

Despite my love for teaching, I recognized that if I wanted to fully commit to academia, there was more to learn. This quest for pedagogical prowess led me to further my education at the University of Pennsylvania—a decision that remains one of the best investments of my life.

The experience deepened my understanding of teaching, reinforcing that prowess is not a destination but a continuous journey. Being at Penn was transformative for me. It reshaped my approach to teaching and solidified my role as a scholar practitioner, committed to blending practical experience with academic rigor.

When I returned to the classroom, I knew I could offer my students a richer, more nuanced learning experience as a scholar practitioner. It's no surprise that my dissertation—focused on teaching prowess and pedagogical effectiveness—earned double distinctions and was accepted into the Library of Congress in Washington, DC.

My mission was clear: to create new pathways that empower both faculty and students in advancing the role of pedagogy and student learning success.

Creating a prowess map gave me the opportunity to look inward—to reflect on who I wanted to become next and identify the actions I needed to take to turn those aspirations into reality.

It's a process that my coauthor, Marshall, describes in his book *Triggers* as the key to creating lasting behavior change and becoming the person you want to be.

With that in mind, we now turn the lens back on you. It's time to ask an important question: where are you on your quest for prowess?

Mapping Out Your Quest for Prowess

Use the personal prowess map shown in Figure 1.2 to reflect on your current situation. Consider the factors that led you to pick up this book, and channel those insights into the spaces provided. Let this exercise be a starting point for your journey toward growth and transformation.

The transformation you seek may be personal or professional—but it begins by crafting a narrative that bridges where you are today with whom you aspire to become. What we refer to as your *desired future self,* we mean the version of you that emerges after engaging deeply with this process— through the personal prowess map or any other path of intentional change.

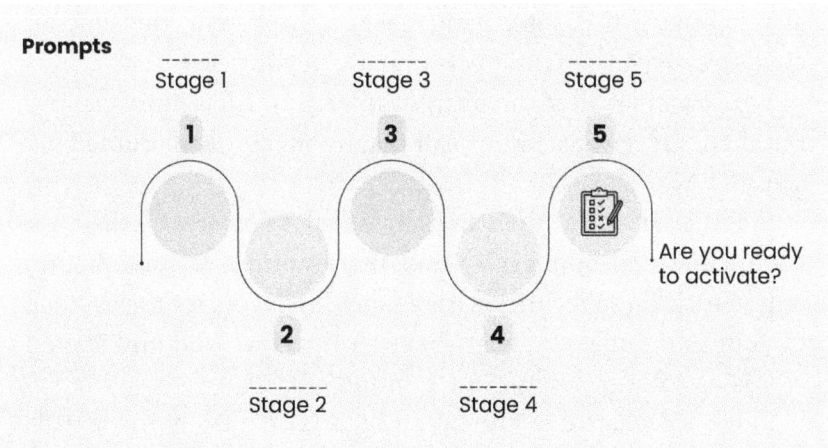

FIGURE 1.2 The personal prowess map.

How to Complete Your Personal Prowess Map: A Step-by-Step Guide

Stage 1. Take a moment to reflect on what's happening around you. What has occurred recently, or what changes are you anticipating? What has sparked your pursuit of growth or ignited your drive for self-improvement? Identify what triggered this journey—an event, experience, or realization—and write it as a label. Summarizing the experience in a word or short phrase can help encapsulate its essence.

Feel free to expand on your thoughts in notes either under the label or in a separate file. While creating a label might feel challenging, it's a meaningful way to distill the experience into something memorable and impactful.

For example, my label was *birth of a child*. What's yours?

Stage 2. Now, reflect on what unfolded afterward or shortly after that experience. Be prepared to lean into vulnerability, but also approach this stage gently, especially if reflecting uncovered sensitive or potentially traumatic memories.

For example, after the birth of my child, I felt immense joy. But then, I received a phone call that momentarily disrupted my sense of calm.

Stage 3. How did the experience make you feel? Reflect on the incident (if applicable) and the emotions it brought up. Summarize these feelings with a label that captures the essence of your emotional response. Below your label, add any related words or emotions that come to mind.

Stage 4. Did anyone say something to you during or after this experience? Whether it was positive or negative, include it in your reflection. Add it to your label and explore its significance.

The goal of this stage is to build your personal prowess map. By reflecting on the incident that triggered your reaction, you can channel the energy from the experience and reframe it in a way that empowers your actions and strengthens your resolve.

Stage 5. What are you willing to do to achieve your desired outcome? Reflect on the steps you must take to move forward. What actions are necessary, and how can you start today?

Several academic theories have closely examined human behavior and motivation, and the personal prowess map exercise is designed to tap into your emotional experiences as a driver for activating your "willingness." This concept is central to the WIN mindset model—the foundation of this book—which emphasizes key actions that can sustain your momentum toward achieving better outcomes and becoming your desired self.

The Prowess Map and Motivation Theories

To align the personal prowess map with well-established theories, we have selected three academic frameworks to better explain this phenomenon.

The first is self-determination theory (SDT), developed by Edward Deci and Richard Ryan in their book *Intrinsic Motivation and Self-Determination in Human Behavior* (Springer, 1985), which emphasizes autonomy, competence, and relatedness as critical psychological needs that drive motivation. When we engage with aspects of SDT, we feel a greater sense of control, choice, autonomy, and capability in our actions.

Our personal prowess map closely aligns with SDT by promoting self-reflection and fostering intrinsic motivation. It mirrors the five core principles of SDT through its staged approach: *clarity* as Stage 1, *challenge* as Stage 2, *acceptance* as Stage 3, *feedback* as Stage 4, and *complexity* as Stage 5.

As shown in Figure 1.3, this progression empowers individuals to take ownership of their growth, enabling intentional and informed choices that lead to meaningful and lasting outcomes.

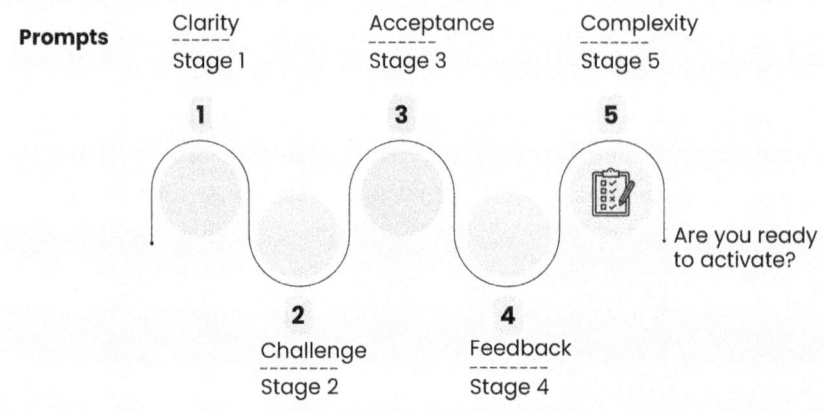

FIGURE 1.3   The personal prowess map and SDT.

The second academic framework, the role of commitment and willingness in goal achievement, based on the work of Edwin Locke and Gary Latham in their book *A Theory of Goal Setting and Task Performance* (Prentice-Hall, 1990), this theory explores the interplay between personal commitment and the willingness to take specific actions necessary to achieve our goals or to set goals. It highlights that willingness acts as a powerful catalyst, transforming abstract intentions into actionable steps that create meaningful outcomes.

This process often unfolds when we experience a range of emotions—joy, hope, or even confusion—while envisioning the possibilities we seek. As we gain clarity on how to move forward, this clarity fuels our motivation and commitment.

Within the context of the personal prowess map, identifying moments of emotional significance helps anchor our intentions, deepen our commitment, and strengthen the willingness to take purposeful steps toward transformation.

The third academic framework, the flow and motivation theory, proposed by Mihaly Csikszentmihalyi in his book *Flow: The Psychology of Optimal Experience* (Harper, 1990), explores how individuals achieve a state of optimal performance and engagement—*flow*—when their skills are perfectly aligned with the challenge they face. This state enhances motivation, productivity, and focus, propelling individuals toward successful outcomes or inspiring them to explore new possibilities.

With the personal prowess map, we can actively create a sense of flow triggered by significant life events or emotional reactions. By documenting these moments, we gain clarity on the flow state—identifying the skills we already possess and the ones we need to develop to reach the next level in our leadership journey.

Embracing Change: The Power of the Personal Prowess Map

By mapping emotional triggers and reframing experiences, the personal prowess map creates clarity about what drives engagement and aligns actions with a renewed sense of purpose. This alignment makes the pursuit of goals more fulfilling and sustainable.

Each of these theories reinforces the idea that *willingness* is a powerful driver of change. They illustrate how aligning emotional experiences with intentional actions can unlock personal growth and guide individuals toward their best selves.

Together, these frameworks enhance the impact of the WIN mindset, making it a transformative tool for achieving long-term success in business and personal lives.

If you have taken the time to complete your personal prowess map, congratulations on this significant milestone! I know it wasn't easy, but it speaks volumes about your self-perception, self-motivation, and willingness to transform.

It's important to recognize that you will have multiple iterations of your personal prowess maps throughout your life, each reflecting your growth and evolving aspirations. You're also invited to return this book for reinforcement and guidance as you step into new horizons.

As we transform, achieve new goals, and navigate disappointments, our desire to do more and redefine our personal prowess maps also evolves. This continuous growth aligns with what Marshall describes as our aspirations, one of the As in the triple A model we discussed in the book's Introduction, and we share the interconnectedness to the personal prowess map in the next section.

The Triple A Model and the Personal Prowess Map

Marshall's triple A model—action, ambition, and aspiration—intertwines seamlessly with my quest for prowess and pursuit of pedagogical effectiveness.

Each component of the triple A model shapes my journey: my action is to improve my teaching, my ambition is to become a scholar practitioner, and my aspiration is to support the university's academic goals, enhance student success, and contribute to faculty development.

This journey of continuous growth has brought me a profound sense of fulfillment, enabling me to engage in academic discussions that extend far beyond the classroom.

The personal prowess map acts as a guiding framework, helping me visualize my progress and align my actions with my ambitions and aspirations. This blend of teaching and consulting fuels my passion and reinforces my commitment to developing my expertise and honing my skills. Returning to the classroom with more to offer my students, fellow faculty, and my program.

My experiences have shaped every aspect of my life, particularly as an educator, leader, and individual. By leveraging the triple A model within the personal prowess map, I can continuously refine my path, enriching my contributions to students and the broader academic community.

In addition to these pursuits, my leadership as the founder of the Global Connections for Women Foundation has had its own trifecta effect: I became a more strategic, decisive, and effective leader. I gained clarity in defining the mission and vision of the foundation and developed strategies for selecting executive board members, staff, and partners to expand our global initiatives. Through this process, I built confidence in my ability to bet on myself and to trust others who shared my vision for supporting humanity.

This leadership journey became a story I shared with the cohorts of female entrepreneurs we trained and developed. Our entrepreneurship programs consistently received 100% satisfaction ratings, with participants often describing the experience as equivalent to taking a business leadership course at Harvard Business School. These outcomes underscored not only the impact of the foundation but also the power of the triple A model in shaping transformative leadership and success.

Aspiration: The Lifelong Pursuit of Prowess

Aspiration is what takes learning and growth beyond the immediate and transforms it into a lifelong pursuit. Aspiration drives us not only to achieve but also to constantly evolve, which is why it's essential to any quest for prowess. Unlike short-term ambition, aspiration embodies our highest goals and deepest values.

As my coauthor, Marshall explains, "Our aspirations may change over time, but they don't disappear," and it is this enduring quality that makes aspiration so powerful—it keeps us striving toward our best selves, even as the destination shifts.

During a podcast interview with Penn GSE, I reflected on our innate desire for prowess and how it manifests in the endless pursuit of an earned life. If you don't take the time to identify and focus on your aspirations, you risk losing the drive that fuels true fulfillment. Without aspirations, life can become centered solely on actions and ambitions, leading to imbalance and a lack of deeper meaning.

Professor Agnes Callard in the book *Earned Life* by Marshall Goldsmith and Mark Reiter (Crown Currency, 2022) refers to this as "aspiring to become knowledgeable." Aspirations drive our desire to learn and continue learning.

Think of a friend, colleague, or family member who has multiple degrees or certifications and who has also self-identified as a professional student.

Being a professional student is admirable if that is who you want to be, but the difference here is understanding that our aspirations drive our desire to learn.

The balance between them enables us to explore the deepest part of ourselves, and learning is the nexus that creates new pathways to expand our strengths into newer territories.

I once gave a keynote address to a room filled with communication executives, where I shared that our instincts can only get us so far because, most often, our instinct is a knee-jerk reaction based on situational underpinnings, which will plateau at some point.

Knowledge serves as the kinetic energy that supports our vision and our drive to create more possibilities and expand our options. Living an earned life means continuously aspiring to achieve something new at every stage of your career.

It's about pursuing growth that brings lasting satisfaction, peace of mind, and joy. For me, this journey has been about investing in myself in ways I never imagined possible.

While aspirations set the direction for our growth, learning prowess provides the tools and mindset necessary to pursue those aspirations effectively.

Connecting Prowess to Action

Aspirations set the direction for our growth, while prowess provides the mindset and tools to pursue those aspirations effectively. When action, ambition, and aspiration align within the prowess map, they create a framework for lasting transformation. By embracing this alignment, we can take ownership of our growth, achieve meaningful goals, and continually strive toward becoming the best version of ourselves.

The Learning Prowess

Learning prowess is deeply personal, and shaped by our mission and purpose. It's about learning effectively and efficiently— acquiring superior knowledge and skills through practice, observation, and both cognitive and emotional engagement.

When executives embrace their learning prowess, and align it with the triple A model, they elevate themselves within their industries, enhance their leadership abilities, and enrich their personal lives.

Aspiration without learning can remain a dream, but when coupled with learning prowess, it becomes a pathway to achieving our highest potential.

In essence, learning prowess is the pursuit of excellence that bridges personal growth with professional fulfillment, serving as the foundation for lasting impact. However, learning prowess demands our full attention and focus—it requires us to be present, intentional, and, above all, willing.

The first pillar of the WIN mindset is the willingness to learn, and it might surprise you how many of us have lost the desire to pursue meaningful learning.

Yet, the quest for prowess cannot manifest without a willingness to engage deeply with the process of learning—a process that not only expands our knowledge but also transforms our personal and professional lives.

So, where do you stand? It's safe to assume that you desire prowess because you've picked up this book. But the bigger question is, "Are you willing to commit to this journey until the very end?"

This is the essence of the learning prowess arc—an ongoing commitment to grow, evolve, and achieve your highest potential, regardless of the circumstances or challenges that trigger your quest for prowess.

In today's world, the word *trigger* is often associated with negative reactions or difficult emotions. However, in this context, a trigger is something entirely different: it represents the spark—the moment or event—that propels you forward on your journey toward learning prowess.

A trigger can be a powerful motivator, awakening your drive to pursue excellence and embrace the growth opportunities that lie ahead. It's not something to avoid; it's something to recognize and harness for positive transformation.

Positive Transformation

When was the last time you experienced a positive transformation? Was it when you treated yourself to something special?

Perhaps when you received a promotion, started your dream job, launched a new business, or made a significant change in your social circle or workplace? Positive transformations come in many forms, big or small.

These moments serve as milestones, reminding us of our capacity to grow, evolve, and reach beyond what we once thought possible. They spark the drive to pursue something greater—or entirely new.

If you want to achieve greatness, ask yourself, "What's stopping me from starting today?"

If you want to fulfill your aspirations, consider, "What steps must I take to bring them to life?"

If you're ready to reimagine your personal and professional future, begin by engaging with your personal prowess map.

Take the time to thoughtfully enter the words, goals, or triggers that will help you access your motivation and chart your path forward.

This book was designed to help you reach your next, most empowered level—one step, one insight, and one intentional action at a time.

2

Investing in Your Prowess: Why It Matters

The Grip of Fear: How It Holds Us Back

The biggest obstacle to investing in oneself is fear. How many opportunities have we missed because fear held us back? Even the bravest among us have felt its grip—racing hearts, sweaty palms, dizziness, anxiety, sleeplessness—those all-too-familiar sensations that come with stepping into the unknown.

Fear is a natural response triggered by the perception of danger, leading to distressing psychological and physical reactions. The *Oxford English Dictionary* defines it as an emotional state marked by discomfort, physiological changes such as increased heart rate and sweating, and a tendency to avoid perceived threats. While fear can sometimes protect us, if left unchecked, it becomes a formidable barrier to growth, success, and self-investment.

When was the last time fear stopped you from reaching beyond your imagination and striving for your true aspirations? Many of us push through fear, enduring its discomfort until we emerge stronger on the other side—a phenomenon that former First Lady Michelle Obama describes as learning to "decode

19

fear" in her book *The Light We Carry* (Crown Publishing, 2022). Yet for many, fear can be paralyzing, causing us to stop short of our aspirations or settle for less than what we truly desire.

Defeating our fears is essential for prowess to manifest, as seen in Figure 2.1. Even when we learn to control or decode our fears, they can still hold us back from taking bold steps toward our goal. Sometimes, it's not even our own fear that holds us back but the projected fear of others—the concerns of a well-meaning parent, spouse, business partner, colleague, or mentor who, in their effort to protect us, unintentionally stifles our growth.

Just as parents instinctively shield their children from harm, these influences can extend beyond childhood, persisting into adulthood in ways that keep us from taking risks and embracing new opportunities.

Recognizing fear for what it is—a common yet often limiting experience—is the first step in overcoming it. By acknowledging and understanding our fears, we gain the power to confront them, freeing ourselves to invest in our prowess and pursue our aspirations with confidence, courage, and clarity with the personal prowess map.

FIGURE 2.1   The climb.

As discussed in Chapter 1, the personal prowess map is not just about examining our internal identities and aligning ourselves with our true desires; it is also about confronting our fears and past traumas.

By leveraging these mental models, we can transform our limitations into stepping stones toward our desired future selves. When fear dictates our actions, we don't just lose opportunities—we risk leaving our potential unrealized.

The longer we hesitate, the greater the gap is between what we are capable of and what we actually accomplish. This gap, the space where unfulfilled dreams and ideas reside, is the true cost of untapped potential.

The Cost of Untapped Potential

The cost of untapped potential is the price we pay when we let fear win. There's a saying that resonates deeply in this context: "Where in the world can you find more people with untapped potential? At the cemetery." While this cannot be scientifically measured without qualitative or quantitative studies, the phrase powerfully reframes our perspective on achievement, highlighting the urgency of realizing our full potential. For many, it is the awareness of our mortality that motivates us to plan, conquer, and manifest our aspirations before our time on Earth runs out.

Denzel Washington, a two-time Academy Award winner, urged students in a keynote speech to "empty out all the clips"— a call to give everything they have in pursuit of their goals and aspirations.

His message reinforces the idea that withholding our talents and ideas out of fear or hesitation is a disservice not only to ourselves but also to the world around us. Now, let's explore the cost of untapped potential—both for individuals and organizations.

According to a study by the Gallup, approximately 70% of employees feel disengaged at work, indicating that a significant number of individuals are not fully using their skills and talents.[1]

This disengagement not only stifles personal growth but also hinders organizational success. Research from Gallup reveals that companies with engaged employees outperform their competitors by 147% in earnings per share, underscoring the financial impact of untapped potential within organizations.[2]

A key driver of both engagement and untapped potential is leadership prowess, a concept we will explore further in Part 2 of this book. When leadership prowess is high within an organization, employee engagement surges, fostering innovation, productivity, and sustained business success.

In fact, McKinsey & Company reports that organizations with strong leadership development programs that supports high performers are 2.2 times more likely to outperform their direct competitors. Companies that prioritize leadership development not only unlock the full potential of their workforce but also achieve double-digit revenue growth, higher employee retention, and greater overall job satisfaction.[3]

The Personal Cost of Untapped Potential

Beyond organizations, consider the personal toll of untapped potential. A Gallup study shows that 85% of employees worldwide are not engaged or are actively disengaged at work, often

---

[1] Gallup. (2013, June 11). Gallup releases new findings on the state of the American workplace.   https://news.gallup.com/opinion/gallup/170570/gallup-releases-new-findings-state-american-workplace.aspx

[2] Gallup. (2012). How employee engagement drives growth. https://news.gallup.com/businessjournal/163130/employee-engagement-drives-growth.aspx

[3] McKinsey & Company. (2023). *The state of organizations 2023*. McKinsey & Company.

due to unchallenged skills, lack of development opportunities, or fear of taking risks.[4] How many brilliant ideas, innovations, or breakthroughs remain unrealized simply because fear holds people back?

Additionally, an article by Harvard Business Review found that only 15% of employees feel they are maximizing their potential at work, with many citing self-doubt and uncertainty as key barriers.[5] How often do we let hesitation dictate our actions, keeping us from stepping fully into our capabilities?

The good news is that fear doesn't have to be a roadblock. The personal prowess map serves as a guide to dismantling these barriers, aligning motivation with intention so we can move forward with purpose. By confronting our fears head-on, we transform them into a driving force—fueling our ambitions and propelling us toward our aspirations.

Bridging the Gap: Knowledge Versus Application

Fear is not the only obstacle. Many of us accumulate knowledge yet struggle to apply it—not just because of hesitation, but sometimes because we don't want to be the smartest one in the room.

The fear of outshining others, challenging the status quo, or stepping into leadership can keep us in a cycle of learning without action. And while we hold back, we watch others claim the promotions, recognition, and opportunities—not

---

[4]Gallup. (2017). *State of the global workplace: High-performing workplace cultures need engaged employees.* Gallup.

[5]Ivcevic, Z., Stern, R., & Faas, A. (2021, May 17). Research: What do people need to perform at a high level? *Harvard Business Review.* https://hbr.org/2021/05/research-what-do-people-need-to-perform-at-a-high-level

necessarily because they know more, but because they were bold enough to act.

A study by the Carnegie Institute of Technology revealed that 85% of job success comes from well-developed soft skills, while only 15% is based on technical knowledge.[6] Despite this, many professionals focus solely on acquiring information without learning how to translate it into action.

The difference between those who achieve great things and those who remain stagnant lies in their willingness to act on what they know. Simply acquiring knowledge is not enough—it must be practiced, refined, and expanded. True mastery comes not from the passive collection of information but also from bold, continuous application.

Prowess goes beyond knowledge—it transforms learning into a living force, driven not by obligation but by an insatiable desire to grow, evolve, and excel.

By bridging the gap between learning and execution, we step into our full potential, making a lasting impact on ourselves and the world around us.

So, we ask you these questions:

- What version of yourself exists in the world today?
- Are you taking proactive steps to uncover and develop your full potential?
- Are you held back by fear—the uncertainty of bold action?

History is filled with individuals who, despite fear, stepped forward with conviction. The true lessons of growth and transformation are found in both the hidden and celebrated

---

[6]Mann, C. R. (1918). A study of engineering education (pp. 106–107). Carnegie Foundation for the Advancement of Teaching. https://www.carnegiefoundation.org/faqs/recently-read-somewhere-carnegie-foundation-report-said-85-persons-job-success-product-interpersonal-skills-15-success-result-technical-knowle/

figures of history—individuals who, despite fear, took bold steps forward. Their courage in the face of uncertainty became the foundation of their success. Now, it's your turn to decide: will fear keep you stagnant, or will you harness your prowess by boldly stepping toward the future you envision?

Hidden Figures: The Power of Investing in Prowess

A powerful example of how bold steps have shaped history comes from the story of *Hidden Figures* and three extraordinary women: Katherine Johnson, Dorothy Vaughan, and Mary Jackson. They weren't just intelligent; they were mathematical prodigies with dreams of applying their expertise in service to America during the space race.

Their journey demonstrates that investing in one's abilities and overcoming fear can lead to groundbreaking achievements and inspire generations to come. Their prowess sustained them, giving them a mission and purpose to achieve their aspirations despite the immense challenges they faced.

Yet, they encountered fear in its most tangible form. They lived in an era when segregation was the law, with separate bathrooms and water fountains reinforcing the barriers between people of color and whites. They faced systemic discrimination that limited their access to critical resources, including being denied entry into laboratories because they were women in a male-dominated field.

Beyond physical segregation, they endured professional isolation: being excluded from high-level discussions, denied recognition for their contributions, and forced to work twice as hard to prove their worth. They navigated workplaces where their voices were often dismissed, their ideas stolen or overlooked, and their career advancements blocked by systemic biases.

Despite these challenges, they persisted. They found ways to learn, innovate, and contribute, even when the system tried to silence them and limit their reach. Their determination not only broke barriers but paved the way for future generations.

Katherine Johnson, despite her exceptional skills, often had to fight to have her calculations acknowledged and accepted by her male colleagues. Notwithstanding, she was recognized to have helped NASA send astronauts to the moon.

Dorothy Vaughan, recognizing the rapid advancement of technology, took it on herself to learn programming languages and advocated for her team's recognition in a workplace that frequently overlooked their contributions.

Mary Jackson, determined to become an engineer, had to petition the court to attend night classes at an all-white school—an extraordinary act of resilience and determination.

Despite these challenges, their commitment to excellence and their refusal to let fear dictate their future ultimately changed the course of history. Their stories serve as proof that when we invest in our prowess and push past fear, we can break through barriers and create lasting impact—not just for ourselves, but for the generations that follow.

Lessons from *Hidden Figures*: Courage in Action

These women refused to let fear dictate their futures. Instead, they challenged limitations, took bold steps forward, and proved that prowess is only as powerful as its application. Their contributions helped shape history.

Katherine Johnson's precise calculations were critical to the success of early NASA missions, including John Glenn's historic orbit around Earth in 1962. Dorothy Vaughan became NASA's first Black female supervisor, mastering the emerging field of computer programming and preparing her team for the shift from human computation to digital computing. Mary Jackson, after breaking racial and gender barriers, became NASA's first Black female engineer in 1958, paving the way for future generations of women in science, technology, engineering, and math fields.

Despite the systemic challenges they faced, these women refused to be confined by the limitations imposed upon them. They adapted, learned, and applied their knowledge, proving that talent and perseverance could break through even the most rigid societal barriers.

Conquering Fear by Investing in Your Prowess

Knowledge is the most powerful tool for conquering fear. Investing in your prowess is an internal soliloquy—one that leadership thinker and my coauthor, Marshall Goldsmith, describes in his first *New York Times* bestselling book, *What Got You Here Won't Get You There*. Growth requires continuous learning and application, along with a willingness to step beyond what is comfortable and familiar.

In that book's chapter titled "You Are Here," Marshall argues that sometimes we lose our internal compass—the guide that helps us navigate our next steps and decisions.

Why do we need an internal compass, you might ask? Because *everyone* needs a guiding force to stay on track, remain accountable, and live with purpose. The absence of direction can leave us feeling stuck, hesitant to move forward, and unsure of our next steps.

So, our question for you is this: where do you want to go next, and how can you apply this model to achieve your objectives?

Before answering this, I want to share my experience working with students of all ages and academic levels. As a learning leader, I have had the good fortune of teaching precollege students, master's degree students, and doctoral candidates.

Across these diverse learning environments, I have noticed a common thread: an initial fear—often openly expressed—when stepping into the classroom. Almost all recognize the importance of investing in their prowess, yet many grapple with imposter syndrome as they engage in their work.

What we have come to understand is that once individuals push past the initial sensation of fear, they often encounter a second challenge: self-doubt. Questions arise: Is this where I am supposed to be? Do I truly deserve this experience? Overcoming fear is only the first step.

The real transformation happens when we acknowledge these doubts and move forward anyway, proving to ourselves that we are more than capable of growing into the roles and opportunities before us.

Lessons from Icons: Overcoming Self-Doubt Through Prowess

Consider the story of J. K. Rowling, the author of the Harry Potter series. Before her success, Rowling faced numerous rejections (from 12 publishers) and experienced profound self-doubt about her writing abilities. Despite these setbacks, she continued to believe in her story and dedicated herself to honing her craft.

Rowling's commitment to learning and refining her writing skills—through workshops, feedback from peers, and relentless practice—highlights the importance of pushing through self-doubt to achieve one's dreams.

Her perseverance ultimately led her to find a publisher willing to take a chance on her work, transforming her passion into a global phenomenon. Her series has sold over 500 million copies worldwide and was a major blockbuster movie success.

Another inspiring example is Oprah Winfrey, who faced significant challenges throughout her early life, including poverty and abuse. Despite these obstacles, she embraced her fears and pursued a career in media.

Oprah often shares how overcoming her self-doubt was a critical step in her journey to becoming a successful television host and media mogul. Throughout her career, she continually invested in her personal growth and learning, seeking out mentors, attending workshops, and gaining experiences that expanded her understanding of the industry and her own potential.

Additionally, we can look to Beyoncé, a global icon who has faced criticism and self-doubt throughout her career. Despite this, she continually pushes herself to grow and evolve as an artist and businessperson. Beyoncé emphasizes the importance of hard work, perseverance, and self-belief in overcoming obstacles.

Her commitment to learning from her experiences—whether through vocal training, choreography classes, or seeking constructive criticism—has enabled her to transform challenges into opportunities.

Her journey demonstrates that embracing fear and self-doubt—while remaining committed to continuous learning—can lead to remarkable achievements and lasting influence. It's no surprise that Teyana Taylor—renowned dancer, singer, actress, director, and entrepreneur—was deeply inspired by her early in her career.

When Beyoncé invited Teyana at 14 years old to teach her the Chicken Noodle Soup dance steps, Teyana later shared with Tina Knowles how that moment left a lasting impression. She realized that Beyoncé's humility and professionalism proved that no one is ever above learning—and that example inspired Teyana to carry herself the same way.

Transforming Personal Growth into Leadership Success

These experiences of overcoming fear and self-doubt translate powerfully into the workplace. As executive coaches, Marshall and I have worked with a wide range of leaders, each facing unique challenges in moving past fear, accepting feedback—whether constructive or critical—and shifting their mindset to one that values continuous learning and growth.

Embracing learning prowess is not just beneficial; it's essential for leadership survival. Leaders who resist growth or shy away from change often struggle to inspire their teams, while those who actively seek knowledge and adapt set the tone for a culture of innovation and resilience. Your team can sense when you lack curiosity, agility, or the willingness to develop—and it directly affects trust, engagement, and performance.

By recognizing the power of the learning mindset, leaders not only elevate their own potential but also empower their teams to do the same. The most effective leaders aren't those who claim to have all the answers, but those who continually seek new insights, challenge their own assumptions, and lead by example in the pursuit of growth.

Following are two scenarios illustrating how individuals can apply these lessons.

Case 1. John is a director of operations for a manufacturing company. He has always struggled with public speaking. Despite his extensive experience and expertise, he often doubts his ability to present ideas confidently to the executive team. Inspired by successful leaders, he decides to confront this fear head-on by enrolling in a public speaking workshop.

After several months of practice and constructive feedback, John gains the confidence to present a new operational efficiency initiative to the executive board. His compelling presentation not only highlights his strategic vision but also earns him recognition for his leadership potential, ultimately leading to a promotion to vice president of operations.

Case 2. Xinyi is a senior marketing director at a technology firm. She frequently experiences imposter syndrome, feeling like she doesn't belong among her highly accomplished colleagues. Despite her impressive qualifications and track record, she worries that she isn't as skilled as her peers.

After attending a leadership development program focused on overcoming self-doubt, Xinyi learns to embrace her unique insights and contributions. She begins to share her innovative ideas more openly in executive meetings, leading to the successful launch of a creative campaign that significantly boosts brand engagement.

Her newfound confidence not only enhances her reputation within the organization but also positions her as a key player in shaping future marketing strategies, resulting in her promotion to chief marketing officer.

■ ■ ■

These scenarios illustrate how confronting fear and self-doubt can lead to personal growth and professional advancement, empowering individuals to thrive in their careers.

My coauthor, Marshall, is famous for reminding us that overcoming fear and self-doubt is an ongoing journey. We need to improve our appetite for embracing 360-degree feedback, committing to behavioral change, and seeking accountability are crucial steps in this process.

By adopting the feed-forward approach, we can focus on future improvements rather than dwelling on past mistakes. Additionally, celebrating small wins along the way can boost our confidence and keep us motivated. As you continue to invest in your prowess and navigate your professional journey, remember that growth is not just about achieving your goals—it's about becoming the leader you aspire to be.

Embracing Learning: The Power of Formal and Informal Approaches

When leaders think about their professional development, they often assume that learning must be formal—and that they simply don't have time for it. However, what truly sets great leaders apart is their commitment to continuous learning and growth.

To fully invest in your development, it's important to understand the balance between formal and informal learning and how both can fit into your busy schedule. Formal learning includes structured programs like courses, certifications, and workshops, while informal learning happens through hands-on experience, peer discussions, and real-world problem-solving.

Meaningful learning is more than just acquiring knowledge—it's about engaging deeply with new ideas, reflecting on experiences, and applying lessons in real time. It is cognitive, experiential, personal, interactive, and practical. When leaders embrace both formal and informal learning, they create environments that foster innovation, collaboration, and continuous improvement.

By integrating these learning strategies, leaders can sharpen their critical thinking, adaptability, and problem-solving skills. This approach not only strengthens personal growth but also enhances leadership impact, retention, and organizational success.

The key is not just making time to learn, but making learning a seamless part of your leadership journey—one that keeps you agile, informed, and ready for the challenges of today's workplace. In today's fast-paced and ever-changing business landscape, effective leadership requires a commitment to continuous learning and adaptation.

Successful leaders recognize that embracing both formal and informal learning opportunities can drive not only their personal growth but also the growth of their teams and organizations.

Successful Leaders Who Embraced Learning and Drove Growth

In today's fast-paced and ever-changing business landscape, effective leadership requires a commitment to continuous learning and adaptation. Successful leaders recognize that embracing both formal and informal learning opportunities can drive not only their personal growth but also the growth of their teams and organizations.

When leaders engage in exploring their prowess, a new level of leadership habits begins to form, including the following:

- **Commitment to continuous learning.** Successful leaders prioritize ongoing education and personal development to stay relevant and effective.
- **Encouraging team growth.** They actively foster an environment where team members feel empowered to pursue their own learning and development.
- **Open communication.** They maintain transparent communication channels that encourage feedback and collaboration among team members.
- **Adaptability.** They demonstrate a willingness to embrace change and adjust their strategies based on new information and insights.
- **Mentorship and coaching.** They invest time in mentoring others, understanding that developing talent within the organization is crucial for long-term success.

To illustrate these habits in action, the following cases showcase how different leaders have harnessed learning to achieve remarkable results, highlighting the profound impact of proactive personal development strategies on organizational success.

Case 1: Investing in Formal Learning to Upskill for Team Growth

Leader: Sarah, VP of marketing at a tech firm

Leadership habit: Commitment to continuous learning

Approach: Sarah enrolled in a leadership development course focused on data-driven decision-making and managing agile teams. She applied her learnings by implementing a new analytics strategy, which helped her team improve campaign performance by 30%. By setting an example, she also encouraged her team members to pursue professional certifications, leading to higher engagement and retention.

Results: As a result of Sarah's initiatives, the marketing team not only improved campaign performance but also experienced increased job satisfaction and a more cohesive team dynamic.

Case 2: Fostering Informal Learning Through Peer-to-Peer Coaching

Leader: Santos, sales director at a consumer product company

Leadership habit: Encouraging team growth

Approach: Rather than relying solely on corporate training, Santos established a peer mentorship program where experienced sales reps coached new hires.

This informal learning approach improved team collaboration and boosted sales performance by 25% within six months, while also reducing turnover by fostering a sense of belonging and community of practice.

Results: Santos's mentorship program led to a stronger team culture, increased sales figures, and higher employee retention rates as new hires felt supported and valued.

Case 3: Obtaining Certification to Drive Organizational Change

Leader: Mary, IT senior manager at a software company

Leadership habit: Commitment to continuous learning

Approach: Mary completed a cybersecurity certification and used her new expertise to develop stronger security protocols. Her proactive learning prevented a potential data breach, saving the company millions. Her leadership also inspired her team to pursue continuous professional development, strengthening overall cybersecurity awareness.

Results: As a result of Mary's initiatives, the company enhanced its security measures, increased employee engagement in professional development programs, and reduced security incidents, leading to improved confidence in the company's cybersecurity posture.

Case 4: Embracing Hands-On Problem Solving for Improvement

Leader: James, chief operating officer (COO) of a fast-growing startup company

Leadership habit: Open communication

Approach: Rather than relying solely on reports, James engaged directly with employees across all departments. Through one-on-one discussions, he identified workflow inefficiencies and introduced agile processes that improved productivity by 40%. His leadership approach strengthened company culture by making employees feel heard and valued.

Results: James's hands-on problem-solving approach resulted in significant productivity gains and increased employee morale, fostering a culture of collaboration and innovation.

Case 5: Developing Staff Through Mentorship Programs

Leader: Elena, director of operations at a logistics company

Leadership habit: Mentorship and coaching

Approach: Elena recognized that her management team was struggling with conflict resolution and team motivation. She implemented a mentorship and leadership coaching program, pairing senior managers with junior team leads. Over six months, employee satisfaction scores increased by 35%, and staff retention rates improved significantly. Her commitment to leadership development strengthened the company's internal talent pipeline.

Results: Elena's mentorship program created a more engaged workforce, reduced turnover, and enhanced the overall effectiveness of the management team, ultimately driving organizational success.

Case Reflection Points: The Power of the Learning Mindset in Leadership

These cases illustrate that effective leadership is rooted in a commitment to continuous learning and a willingness to adapt. By embracing both formal and informal learning opportunities, leaders can foster an environment that promotes growth, innovation, and collaboration.

The key leadership habits identified—commitment to continuous learning, encouraging team growth, open communication, adaptability, and mentorship—are essential for driving not only personal success but also the success of their teams and organizations. As leaders continue to explore their prowess and apply these habits, they empower themselves and their teams to navigate challenges and seize opportunities in an ever-evolving business landscape.

The Flip Side: Leaders Who Took Shortcuts and Failed

By contrast, the following cases illustrate the risks of neglecting continuous learning and the consequences of relying solely on past experiences. These leaders faced significant challenges due to their decisions to bypass essential training and development, ultimately affecting their teams and organizations negatively.

Case 1: Ignoring Learning by Relying Solely on Experience

Leader: Lisa, manufacturing plant executive manager

Error in judgment: Lisa dismissed the need for training on new technology, assuming that her years of experience were enough. When automation tools were introduced, her team struggled to adapt, leading to production delays and costly errors. Employee frustration grew, resulting in higher turnover.

Missing Leadership Habits

- **Commitment to continuous learning.** Lisa's reliance on past experience prevented her from recognizing the need for ongoing education and skills development.
- **Adaptability.** Her unwillingness to adapt to new technologies left her team ill-prepared for change.

Case 2: Implementing Changes Without Sufficient Knowledge

Leader:	Tom, CEO of a mid-sized tech retail firm
Error in judgment:	Tom rushed to implement a remote work policy without studying best practices or consulting his employees. The lack of clear guidelines led to communication breakdowns, lower productivity, and widespread dissatisfaction. Eventually, top talent left for companies with better-structured remote work policies.

Missing Leadership Habits

- **Open communication.** Tom failed to engage his team in the decision-making process, which contributed to confusion and discontent.
- **Adaptability.** His haste to implement changes without adequate research demonstrated a lack of adaptability in addressing the evolving work environment.

Case 3: Failing to Address Employee Development Needs

Leader:	Mark, regional manager at a retail chain conglomerate
Error in judgment:	Mark ignored the importance of employee training and development, assuming that staff would learn

on the job. Over time, his team became disengaged, leading to high turnover, poor customer service ratings, and declining sales. When exit interviews revealed that employees felt unsupported in their growth, leadership was forced to overhaul their entire training strategy to rebuild morale.

Missing Leadership Habits

- **Encouraging team growth.** Mark's neglect of employee development fostered an environment where staff felt undervalued and unsupported.
- **Mentorship and coaching.** His failure to invest in mentoring and coaching prevented team members from reaching their full potential and contributed to disengagement.

Case 4: Overlooking the Importance of Employee Feedback

Leader: Rachel, COO at a health care organization

Error in judgment: Rachel implemented new operational procedures without seeking input from frontline staff. Her decision was based on her belief that she understood the challenges faced by employees, but she did not take the time to gather their insights. As a result, the new procedures were impractical and led to confusion and frustration among staff. Employee morale declined, and patient care suffered due to inconsistent practices.

Missing Leadership Habits

- **Open communication.** Rachel's failure to communicate effectively with her team prevented valuable feedback from being incorporated into the decision-making process.
- **Encouraging team growth.** By not involving employees in the development of new procedures, she missed an opportunity to empower them and foster a sense of ownership over their work.

Case 5: Neglecting to Foster a Culture of Continuous Improvement

Leader: Alex, regional vice president at a private retail chain

Error in judgment: Alex focused solely on immediate sales targets and neglected to invest in training programs that promoted continuous improvement among staff. He believed that prioritizing short-term profits was the best approach, but this lack of emphasis on employee development led to stagnant skills and outdated practices within the team. As a result, customer service suffered, and sales began to decline. When competitor stores introduced better-trained staff and enhanced service experiences, Alex's team struggled to keep up.

Missing Leadership Habits

- **Commitment to continuous learning.** Alex's short-sightedness in ignoring the need for ongoing training hindered the professional growth of his team.
- **Mentorship and coaching.** By failing to provide guidance and development opportunities, he missed the chance to cultivate a high-performing workforce capable of adapting to changing market demands.

Case Reflection Point: Lessons Learned from Leadership Failures

The cases of leaders who took shortcuts and faced setbacks serve as cautionary tales about the perils of neglecting continuous learning and development. Their experiences highlight the importance of cultivating key leadership habits, such as commitment to ongoing education, encouraging team growth, maintaining open communication, embracing adaptability, and investing in mentorship.

By recognizing and addressing these missing habits, current and aspiring leaders can avoid similar pitfalls and create a thriving organizational culture that fosters resilience, innovation, and sustained success. Ultimately, effective leadership requires a willingness to learn, adapt, and empower others, ensuring that both leaders and their teams can navigate the complexities of today's business landscape with confidence.

As demonstrated by both the successes and failures outlined in these cases, the journey of leadership is one of continuous growth, requiring vigilance and dedication to both personal and professional development.

Final Reflections on Investing in Your Prowess and Leadership Success

Successful leaders actively embrace both formal and informal learning opportunities to drive growth, improve team performance, and cultivate a thriving company culture.

By investing in their own prowess, they not only enhance their skill sets but also model the importance of continuous improvement for their teams. By contrast, leaders who neglect learning or take shortcuts expose their organizations to inefficiencies, poor decision-making, burnout, and increased employee turnover.

The most effective leaders understand that making learning a continuous and integrated part of their leadership journey is essential; this approach ensures they remain agile and adaptable in an ever-evolving workplace.

By fostering a culture of learning and demonstrating key leadership habits—such as commitment to continuous learning, encouraging team growth, maintaining open communication, embracing adaptability, and investing in mentorship—leaders can significantly enhance their impact, strengthen their teams, and contribute to long-term organizational success.

Moreover, facing one's fears and overcoming challenges is a vital aspect of effective leadership. By drawing inspiration from others who have navigated similar obstacles, leaders can cultivate resilience and determination.

This mindset not only empowers them to achieve their goals but also inspires their teams to embrace growth and strive for excellence in their own pursuits. Ultimately, investing in one's prowess is not just an individual endeavor; it creates a ripple effect that fosters a culture of success and continuous learning throughout the organization.

3 How Does Continuous Learning Build Credibility?

Scientia Potentia Est Means "Knowledge Is Power"

How many times have you heard, read, or listened to someone say the famous phrase, "knowledge is power," or *scientia potentia est*. Have you ever wondered who first coined this phrase, what motivated them to say it, and how it was received?

The phrase is widely attributed to Sir Francis Bacon, an English philosopher, statesman, scientist, and writer who lived during the late 16th and early 17th centuries (1561–1626). Born in London, Bacon was a key figure in developing the scientific method and the intellectual movement known as the Age of Enlightenment. His work laid the foundation for empirical research, advocating for observation and experimentation to acquire knowledge.

During Bacon's time, Europe was undergoing significant transformation. The Renaissance had revived interest in classical learning, but knowledge was still primarily controlled by the Church and monarchy. Many institutions resisted new ideas that challenged traditional authority. When Bacon asserted that "knowledge is power," he was not merely making a philosophical statement—he advocated for a shift in how knowledge was acquired, used, and distributed. Initially, this was a radical idea, for it suggested that power should come from understanding the world rather than just birthright or religious doctrine.

Bacon's ideas on democratizing knowledge helped pave the way for the Scientific Revolution, leading to groundbreaking discoveries in physics, medicine, and technology. By encouraging empirical research, Bacon's philosophy inspired other scientists, including Isaac Newton, whose laws of motion transformed our understanding of the universe. The embrace of knowledge also led to improved literacy rates, greater access to education, and the foundation of modern universities that continue to fuel innovation today.

Beyond science, embracing knowledge led to higher literacy rates, greater access to education, and the foundation of modern universities that continue to fuel innovation today. The shift toward valuing knowledge and critical thinking played a crucial role in shaping democracy, economic development, and technological progress, proving that knowledge, when applied, is indeed a powerful force for change.

A Radical Idea: How the World First Reacted

At first, Bacon's ideas were met with skepticism, especially by those who benefited from the status quo. The concept gained traction among scholars, scientists, and political thinkers who saw the potential of knowledge to drive progress. One of the most notable leaders who embraced this thinking was Thomas Jefferson, one of the founding fathers of the United States.

Jefferson strongly believed in the power of education to shape a democratic society. His vision for public education and the creation of institutions like the University of Virginia reflected the belief that knowledge should not be limited to the privileged but should empower all citizens.

The acceptance of Bacon's philosophy contributed to the rise of public education systems, scholarship, research, and inductive reasoning—ensuring that knowledge was no longer confined to the elite, bound by tradition, or shaped by untested ideas and the idols of the past.

This democratization of learning contributed to the spread of democracy, social mobility, and economic growth. Over time, access to knowledge empowered individuals to challenge oppression, advocate for civil rights, and innovate in fields ranging from engineering to medicine. Organizations throughout history have interpreted knowledge is power in different ways.

Positive Outcomes of Embracing Knowledge

Businesses that prioritize knowledge and innovation have led some of the most transformative advancements of our time—from the creation of the internet to the rise of artificial intelligence. Likewise, governments that invest in education, research, and public learning cultivate stronger economies, deepen civic engagement, and nurture more informed, resilient societies. Access to knowledge has also powered some of the world's most influential social movements. From civil rights to climate activism, informed individuals have harnessed what they know to advocate for justice, fairness, and sustainability.

The phrase "knowledge is power" is more than a statement—it's a call to action. It challenges us to transform understanding into meaningful impact. Because power doesn't come simply from knowing—it comes from applying what we know wisely, ethically, and purposefully.

For example, Apple Inc. is a company that has consistently transformed knowledge into breakthrough innovation. Through its investment in research, design thinking, and user insights, Apple has reshaped entire industries—from personal computing to mobile technology. Its success is rooted not just in technological brilliance but also in a culture that values continuous learning, iteration, and the bold application of knowledge to meet evolving human needs.

Beyond its cutting-edge products, Apple's long-term success is built on how it attracts, cultivates, and retains talent. The company intentionally fosters a culture of curiosity, creativity, and excellence—where learning is embedded into daily work, and employees are empowered to challenge norms.

Apple is known to invest heavily in design thinking, user research, and cross-functional collaboration, creating an environment where applied knowledge fuels everything from product development to customer experience. Its ability to turn insight into action is not accidental—it's cultural.

On an individual level, former president Barack Obama exemplifies how knowledge can shape a leadership legacy. His journey—from community organizer to the presidency—was powered by deep learning, reflection, and a commitment to civic engagement. Obama has often credited books, education, and listening to everyday people as instrumental in shaping his worldview. He applied this knowledge to bridge divides, lead with empathy, and inspire movements rooted in hope and transformation. His story reminds us that knowledge, when paired with purpose and action, can change lives—and nations.

So, we ask you these questions:

- What are you doing with your knowledge?
- What insights have you gained?
- How have those insights shaped your path, your choices, your growth?

- And just as important, where do you still need to grow?
- Who will benefit from your knowledge, and how will it transform you—your work, your relationships, and your life?

Remember the personal prowess map from Chapter 1: a framework for identifying and investing in the areas of your personal and professional development that matters most. Embracing this commitment to learning and growth doesn't just build capacity—it builds credibility. When used with intention, knowledge becomes the engine behind your influence, your leadership, and your legacy. It drives better decisions, stronger business outcomes, and more productive actions. The more you know, the more prepared you are to navigate the complexities of everyday life and withstand the forces that try to steer you off course. Knowledge is your ship. Credibility is your strength. And that strength propels you—and those you lead—toward newer horizons, through challenges, and into new frontiers.

First Comes Knowledge, Then Comes Trust and Credibility

If you're reading this and asking yourself, "How is knowledge connected to credibility?"—you're in the right place. That question signals curiosity, and curiosity is the first step in unlocking the real power of the learning mindset. As you move through this book, you'll see how gaining and applying knowledge not only empowers you but also builds trust, authority, and influence in every aspect of your life.

Credibility isn't just about what you know—it's about how consistently and confidently you use that knowledge to make sound decisions, support others, and lead with integrity. In leadership, credibility earns you influence. In communication, it earns you trust. In your career, it opens doors. When others recognize that your knowledge is grounded in insight and action, not just theory, they're more likely to listen, collaborate, and follow your lead. Simply put: the more you invest in learning and applying what you know, the more credible—and powerful—you become.

Take Dr. Kizzmekia Corbett, a lead scientist in the development of the Moderna COVID-19 vaccine. Before the pandemic, she was mostly unknown outside of scientific circles. But her years of research in immunology—and her ability to communicate that science clearly—helped build a life-saving solution and public trust. Her credibility wasn't just based on credentials; it came from applying knowledge under pressure, collaborating across sectors, and educating with clarity and compassion.

Her professional story reminds us that when paired with purpose and action, knowledge can change the world—and earn the credibility to lead through crises and otherwise. You might say, "Of course, a scientist is a lifelong learner—that's part of the job." And that's true.

But to think that only scientists need to learn deeply is to overlook the power of your own learning mindset and your personal journey. Every one of us has a sphere of influence. To fully step into yours, you must be willing to learn, grow, and trust that your actions matter. Knowledge, when applied with purpose, becomes the foundation of credibility—in work, in leadership, and in life.

When Knowledge Increase Access to Credibility

Marshall Goldsmith and I have had the privilege of working with professionals at pivotal moments in their careers—individuals who don't just acquire knowledge but also apply it intentionally to elevate their performance, empower their teams, and create balance across all areas of life.

Their journeys remind us of a simple truth: everyone has something to give, and your knowledge is powerful, too. However, the pursuit of knowledge is the gateway to increasing one's credibility, expertise, and ability.

As your expertise grows and your ability to apply it deepens, people begin to look to you—not just for answers, but for guidance, perspective, and leadership. You become a trusted voice, a go-to resource, and someone others rely on to navigate complexity and drive results. That credibility opens doors, amplifies your influence, and shapes how people engage with your ideas and actions, as leaders within an organization.

But remember—do it not for credibility, but in spite of it. When leaders create space to show up as their authentic selves, it's rarely about seeking recognition. Recognition becomes the by-product of consistency, perseverance, and purpose-driven action.

Credibility, however, doesn't arrive with a degree, a job title, or even years of experience. It is earned through consistent learning and thoughtful application. When you demonstrate that your knowledge translates into clear decisions, meaningful contributions, and thoughtful leadership, others begin to trust in your ability to deliver—not just once, but over time.

Across industries, we see organizations that invest in learning at both the individual and collective levels to cultivate credibility, trust, and sustainable success. These environments don't just produce high performers; they create resilient cultures where learning drives adaptation, innovation, and long-term impact.

Learning in Action: Learning Builds Leadership, Culture, and Results

In today's fast-changing world, organizations that prioritize meaningful learning empower leaders and teams to adapt, innovate, and deliver lasting impact. The following three examples showcase how investing in purposeful learning drives not only individual growth but also transforms workplace culture and business outcomes.

First is Airbnb, a company that understands the value of shared experiences and relational travel. During its rapid expansion, Airbnb focused not only on business growth but also on developing leaders who could translate global complexity into local impact.

Through internal programs focused on cultural intelligence, ethical decision-making, and customer empathy, Airbnb equipped its teams to lead thoughtfully across diverse markets. They believed in transformational leadership, a multiplier in shaping the culture where leadership and care was visible.

The results accounted for their consistency in brand experience, adaptability, and market growth. The company's investment in knowledge-sharing and team-based learning built trust internally and externally, strengthening brand reputation, accelerating decision-making, and ensuring that expansion was sustainable and values-driven.

For Airbnb, empowering their leaders with the right tools to expand their knowledge also directly affected the credibility of their brand—a win-win scenario for both the leaders and the business.

Second is Microsoft. Most times, building credibility through knowledge must be reinforced at the top—and in this scenario, that leadership came from Satya Nadella, CEO of Microsoft. Nadella's leadership marked a philosophical shift at Microsoft: from a static culture of expertise to a dynamic culture of learning.

By encouraging a "learn-it-all" mindset and modeling vulnerability in leadership, Nadella inspired employees to embrace feedback, challenge assumptions, and experiment boldly.

The results were a cultural shift that not only served the organization but also benefitted both internal and external stakeholders. This change reignited innovation, transformed team dynamics, and positioned Microsoft as a forward-thinking tech giant.

Nadella's credibility as a leader didn't stem solely from his technical prowess—it was reinforced by his humility, learning orientation, and ability to align people on shared growth.

The third example is IBM. Facing a rapidly evolving digital landscape, IBM made a strategic bet on its people. Through initiatives like SkillsBuild and Think40, IBM fostered a learning-first culture where upskilling was tied directly to performance and advancement. Employees weren't just encouraged to learn—they were expected to.

With Think40, employees were expected to commit to 40 hours of learning and development per year, and twice the amount was often reported. Why? In part because their personal prowess map was built into the technology, when employees were able input their current job title and set specific skills-related goals.

The results were not surprising when the focus shifted to people over other business priorities. Their learning programs and culture strengthened IBM's workforce, improved employee engagement, and positioned the company to stay relevant in a fast-moving market.

Managers gained credibility by modeling growth and leading by example, creating teams that were agile, collaborative, and future ready. The SkillsBuild platform is also open to everyone and everywhere, expanding their learning culture outside of its domain.

Culture Drives Learning

When workplace culture is grounded in shared values, beliefs, behaviors, and practices, it shapes how people interact, make decisions, and collaborate. This culture forms the invisible framework that guides everything from daily tasks and team dynamics to strategic goals and innovation.

A culture that actively supports continuous learning—balancing structured, required learning with individualized, self-directed development—creates an environment where people feel empowered to grow, share knowledge, and think creatively. In such environments, individuals evolve not only into stronger contributors but also into catalysts for innovation and stewards of a learning mindset.

Here, learning isn't a one-off initiative—it's embedded in the fabric of the organization. It fuels both personal growth and collective advancement, unlocking the true power of knowledge by integrating it into everyday behaviors and decisions.

It's no wonder that management expert Peter Drucker famously said, "Culture eats strategy for breakfast." The critical role of workplace culture in advancing learning prowess is central to executing—and sustaining—a growth strategy. At the organizational level, even the most brilliant strategy will falter without a strong, aligned culture to support it. At the individual level, no matter how much knowledge you've acquired or how steep your learning curve, it's the culture that determines whether you can apply, grow, and lead.

So, what is your workplace culture? How would you describe it? What would your team say—and would their answers align with yours?

If you can answer those questions confidently and consistently, your culture is likely aligned with your learning goals.

But if your confidence varies from question to question, that signals an opportunity for improvement.

Here's the truth: you help shape the culture the moment you walk in. You carry the responsibility of advocating for a workplace that prioritizes learning—not just through traditional learning and development teams that equip employees with job-related knowledge but also through a culture that nurtures aspirations, leadership potential, and the pursuit of learning as a lifelong journey.

The trifecta effect—individual growth, team empowerment, and organizational excellence—depends on a learning-focused culture. Your prowess map might ultimately reflect your desire to cultivate a workplace culture where learning is not an afterthought but a driving force behind long-term success.

The following examples highlight how leaders across different sectors have championed learning cultures—and how you can do the same:

- **Satya Nadella, CEO of Microsoft.** On becoming CEO in 2014, Satya Nadella transformed Microsoft's culture from a "know-it-all" to a "learn-it-all" mindset. He emphasized empathy, collaboration, and a growth mindset throughout the organization. This cultural shift was pivotal in revitalizing Microsoft's innovation and performance.
- **Rosalind Brewer, former CEO of Walgreens Boots Alliance.** Rosalind Brewer was the first woman to ever be the CEO in that role, and while she was at Walgreens Boots Alliance, she prioritized inclusive leadership and employee development during her tenure. She encouraged leaders to actively listen to employees and fostered environments where continuous learning and diversity of thought were valued.

- **Alan Mulally, former CEO of Ford Motor Company.** Alan Mulally led Ford through a significant cultural transformation by implementing the "business plan review" process. This weekly meeting promoted transparency, accountability, and collective problem-solving, embedding continuous learning into the company's operations.

These examples demonstrate that cultivating a learning culture requires intentional leadership, structured opportunities, and an environment where growth is valued over perfection.

10 Habits to Cultivate a Learning Culture

As you refine your own prowess map, consider the conditions you're creating to ensure that your people—and your organization—can learn, grow, and thrive. Do so in a way that aligns with your authentic self and reflects the true potential of your team and organization—bridging the space between where you are today and where you aspire to grow. Leading experts in workplace learning and organizational development— such as Nigel Paine, a global thought leader and author who helps organizations transform learning cultures; Josh Bersin, a renowned industry analyst and researcher in human resources and talent management; Amy Edmondson, Harvard Business School professor and pioneer of psychological safety; and Mark Thompson, a CEO executive coach focused on cultivating high-impact leaders—emphasize that building a thriving learning culture depends on intentional habits practiced by leaders. Drawing from their insights and ours, these habits create the conditions that empower individuals and teams to continuously grow, innovate, and drive collective success.

Let's explore the 10 habits to help you cultivate and sustain a learning-focused workplace culture.

Habit 1: Model Continuous Learning

Leaders set the tone for the entire organization by actively demonstrating curiosity, humility, and a commitment to growth. When leaders show that they are continuously learning—adapting, evolving, and acknowledging what they don't yet know—they normalize and elevate learning as a core organizational value. But modeling isn't just about personal development; it's also about prioritizing learning for others.

Leaders must help identify what the organization needs to learn and evolve, and they must create space and time for their teams to grow. When leaders consistently invest in their own learning and advocate for their team's development, learning becomes both visible and valued across the organization.

Habit 2: Create Psychological Safety

People need to feel safe to express ideas, ask questions, and make mistakes without fear of judgment or reprisal. Psychological safety fosters open dialogue, innovation, and genuine learning—all essential for continuous improvement and team growth.

Success relies on a steady flow of fresh ideas, meaningful challenges, and critical thinking—none of which can thrive in an environment where people feel silenced, ridiculed, or intimidated. If you notice a gap in psychological safety on your team, start by identifying where it exists and build from that place with intention.

Invite your team into the process. Encourage collective ownership in discovering how to deepen psychological safety and how to cultivate it as a team norm and organizational value.

Active participation and honest feedback are crucial to making this a shared and lasting practice.

And remember—you don't have to do it alone. Bring in your team or seek external support to help facilitate the process. Psychological safety isn't built in isolation; it's modeled, reinforced, and sustained through consistent leadership behaviors and shared commitment.

Habit 3: Hold Leadership Accountable for Learning Culture

Leaders must take ownership of creating and sustaining a culture where learning is prioritized. Accountability ensures that learning is not treated as an optional extra but as a vital component of team and organizational success. When leaders are evaluated not just on outcomes but also on how they support growth and learning in others, it sends a powerful message. A culture of learning thrives when leadership is not only committed to development but held responsible for modeling, reinforcing, and enabling it—encouraging others to do the same.

Habit 4: Align Learning with Purpose and Strategy

Learning initiatives should be directly connected to the organization's mission, values, and strategic goals. When employees understand how their development efforts contribute to larger objectives, learning becomes more relevant and motivating. Alignment fosters not just skill building, but purpose-driven engagement. This may also mean learning from within—by staying attuned to internal shifts, crises, and emerging priorities. In these moments, effective leaders lean in, assess what the organization needs most, and create a pathway for their teams to adapt and grow. Whether it's navigating a challenge or sustaining momentum, learning becomes the bridge between current realities and future success.

Habit 5: Embed Learning in Daily Work

Learning is most effective when it's contextual—woven into the tasks, decisions, and reflections of everyday work. Rather than being reserved for formal training sessions or special events, learning should be integrated into the daily rhythm of team life. This habit requires a systematic approach and a leadership commitment to building a culture where learning is expected, supported, and scheduled—not seen as a disruption. The most effective way to embed this habit is to ensure that your team feels empowered and supported when learning opportunities arise during their regular work. That support may include protected time, tools for reflection, or access to just-in-time resources. When learning becomes a natural part of how work gets done, it fuels both immediate performance and long-term growth.

Habit 6: Empower Autonomy and Self-Direction

Individuals learn best when they have the autonomy to pursue topics and methods aligned with their personal goals, interests, and growth areas. This sense of ownership over one's development enhances engagement, strengthens motivation, and fosters loyalty and retention, ensuring that learning remains relevant, personalized, and impactful.

Leaders play a critical role in this process by asking team members what additional resources they need to thrive and actively advocating for access to those resources. Organizations should go further by sponsoring external learning opportunities, such as certificate programs, postgraduate courses, conferences, workshops, or webinars.

This isn't about discretionary funding that can be easily withheld or deprioritized. It's a strategic investment in talent. When organizations commit to financially supporting the learning and development of their people, they strengthen performance, boost retention, and signal that growth is not just encouraged, but expected and supported. After all, everyone wants to be successful in their role and create meaningful value. Leaders who champion this kind of investment help unlock that potential.

Habit 7: Encourage Experimentation and Innovation

A culture that rewards trying new approaches—even when outcomes are uncertain—drives creativity, adaptability, and resilience. Experimentation is a powerful form of learning, helping teams test ideas, challenge assumptions, and evolve through insight.

In today's fast-changing environments, results are often harder to predict due to increased complexity and ambiguity. Rather than allowing fear or indecision to stall progress, encourage your team to carve out time to test ideas and pilot new solutions.

Make experimentation a shared, vocal process: normalize conversations about confidence levels, alternative paths, and even fears about taking action. When leaders champion this openness, they foster a culture where innovation thrives, and where learning is continuous, courageous, and aligned with the organization's evolving needs.

Habit 8: Foster Collaboration and Knowledge Sharing

Breaking down silos unlocks diverse perspectives and fuels collective problem-solving. When teams share insights openly and consistently, learning accelerates and innovation becomes a shared outcome.

However, when workplace culture promotes intense internal competition, knowledge hoarding becomes the norm—undermining trust, collaboration, and ultimately, sustainable growth.

To foster a learning culture, shift from competition to collaboration. Create space for teams to inspire one another rather than compete for recognition or resources. Celebrate shared expertise and encourage the mindset that when one person learns or solves a problem, the whole team benefits.

This doesn't mean eliminating all competition—healthy competition can drive performance—but unchecked rivalry erodes unity and slows progress. By contrast, cultures that promote fierce inspiration over fierce competition empower people to contribute freely, support one another, and grow together.

Celebrate shared expertise as a symbol of leadership and collaboration, not as a threat. While healthy competition can spark motivation, unchecked rivalry fractures teams, stifles learning, and leads to talent loss and stagnation.

A true learning culture prioritizes connection, contribution, and collective success above all.

Habit 9: Communicate Transparently and Frequently

Clear, open communication about learning goals and progress keeps everyone informed, engaged, and aligned. Transparency builds trust and ensures that learning efforts are both visible and valued.

Continuous learning also builds credibility—especially when leaders openly share what they're learning, what's changing, and why it matters. This habit becomes mutually beneficial to leaders, teams, and the organization as a whole. It signals that learning is not just encouraged but also embedded in how the organization operates.

There should be intentional spaces within an organization where transparent dialogue—especially about complexities, missteps, or uncertainty—is welcomed and respected. Transparency fuels a growth mindset, strengthens cultural alignment, and drives performance by making it safe to learn, adapt, and improve together.

Habit 10: Recognize and Reward Learning and Growth

Acknowledging and celebrating learning achievements inspires continued effort and reinforces a culture where growth is both expected and appreciated. Recognition sends a clear message: development is not only encouraged—it's essential to the success of individuals and the organization.

A meaningful example of this habit in action occurred during a graduation ceremony at Columbia University, School of Professional Studies. Dean Troy Eggers not only honored the graduating class of 2025 but also paused to acknowledge staff members and faculty in the audience who had pursued their professional development. When asked why he did this, his response reflected the essence of this habit: recognizing learning at all levels demonstrates support for growth and signals that every step toward development is valued.

Whether it's a formal celebration or a personal acknowledgment, leaders who recognize learning create a culture where progress is visible, meaningful, and worth striving for.

Leadership Missteps Versus Leadership Wins

To help bring these habits to life, let's explore real-world leadership scenarios that show the difference between approaches that hold teams back versus those that empower and inspire growth. Each example highlights how small shifts in mindset and behavior can transform your workplace culture and accelerate learning for everyone.

Habit 1: Model Continuous Learning

Leadership misstep. At Company A, the chief financial officer rarely attends training or engaged in new industry trends. He expects his team to keep up but does not invest time in learning himself. This attitude signals that learning isn't a priority, causing disengagement and stagnation in skills across the department.

Leadership win. At Company B, the chief technology officer regularly shares books, attends conferences, and openly discusses what she's learning. She sets aside time weekly for personal development and encourages her team to do the same. This approach fosters curiosity and motivates the team to stay ahead in a fast-evolving market increasing their desire to attend conferences.

Habit 2: Create Psychological Safety

Leadership misstep. During team meetings at Company C, the manager dismisses ideas that seemed risky and subtly criticizes mistakes. Team members become reluctant to speak up, fearing embarrassment. Innovation stalls, and problems have been hidden until they escalated. Team morale has been low, but the manager doesn't even notice, unfortunately.

Leadership win. At Company D, the department head actively invites diverse opinions and frames failures as learning opportunities. She thanks team members for sharing different perspectives, creating an environment where people feel safe to take risks and learn openly. Here, the team morale was at its highest level, and the openness to feedback made the team feel at ease with their leader.

Habit 3: Hold Leadership Accountable for Learning Culture

Leadership misstep. At Company E, executives talk about learning but do not allocate resources or time for it. When teams miss learning goals, no one addresses it. Leaders don't model or reward learning behaviors, so it's viewed as optional rather than essential. There was a longing to learn and grow, but the restrictive culture made it difficult and uncomfortable to even bring it up. So, everyone remains quiet and continues work as usual with little or no access to learning, development, or mentors.

Leadership win. At Company F, the CEO includes learning objectives in executive performance reviews and publicly celebrates leaders who champion development. This accountability drives a culture where continuous learning is embedded in everyone's responsibilities.

Habit 4: Align Learning with Purpose and Strategy

Leadership misstep. At Company G, learning programs are generic and disconnected from employees' day-to-day roles or company goals. There is very limited connection to employees' goals and aspirations. Participation is low, and employees struggle to see the value in the training, leading to wasted resources. While the design of this workplace teaches their employees what they should learn without consultation, everyone has gone with the flow. This is a common scenario in most organizations, where learning and development has been secondary in priority and importance.

Leadership win. At Company H, learning initiatives are designed for strategic priorities like sustainability and innovation. Teams understand how their development contributes directly to the company's mission, resulting in higher engagement and impactful outcomes.

Habit 5: Embed Learning in Daily Work

Leadership misstep. At Company I, training has been treated as a separate activity scheduled sporadically. Employees find it hard to balance learning with their workload, so skills development often gets postponed or ignored.

Leadership win. At Company J, managers integrate microlearning, on-the-job coaching, and reflection into daily routines. Learning becomes a natural part of work, enhancing skills without sacrificing productivity.

Habit 6: Empower Autonomy and Self-Direction

Leadership misstep. At Company K, leadership dictates all learning opportunities without consulting their teams. Employees quickly become disengaged, as the training fails to align with their interests or professional growth goals. As a result, many begin seeking new opportunities at organizations that prioritize and support individual learning and development.

Leadership win. At Company L, leaders ask their teams about learning preferences and support personalized development plans, including funding external courses and certifications. This autonomy boosts motivation, retention, and aligns growth with both individual and organizational goals.

Habit 7: Encourage Experimentation and Innovation

Leadership misstep. At Company M, risk-averse leaders punish mistakes harshly. Employees avoid trying new methods, leading to repetitive work and missed opportunities for improvement.

Leadership win. At Company N, leaders celebrate thoughtful experiments and openly discuss lessons learned from failures.

Teams feel encouraged to innovate, leading to creative solutions and increased agility.

Habit 8: Foster Collaboration and Knowledge Sharing

Leadership misstep. At Company O, fierce competition between teams has led to siloed information and withheld insights. This causes duplicated work, delayed problem-solving, and internal distrust, ultimately stifling innovation and increasing employee turnover.

Leadership win. At Company P, the CEO has shifted focus to collaboration by promoting shared goals and regular knowledge sharing. Teams work together more effectively, solve problems faster, and generate innovative ideas. Trust and morale have improved, boosting retention and sustainable growth.

Habit 9: Communicate Transparently and Frequently

Leadership misstep. At Company Q, leadership has launched a professional development program without clearly connecting it to career growth or company goals. Managers lack talking points, and employees are left unsure if participation matters. Engagement has dropped, and many have seen the effort as performative. In exit interviews, employees cite unclear learning expectations as a reason for leaving.

Leadership win. At Company R, leaders prioritize clear communication about learning. Quarterly town halls highlight development goals and celebrate progress, while managers use check-ins to align learning with performance and growth. Employees understand how learning affects their careers, boosting trust, engagement, and retention. As one team lead put it,

"We don't guess what matters—our leaders make it clear that learning is the work."

Habit 10: Recognize and Reward Learning and Growth

Leadership misstep. At Company S, employees have been encouraged to complete online certifications and attend skills training programs, but their efforts went unnoticed. There were no acknowledgments in team meetings, performance reviews, or internal communications. Over time, employees have begun to feel that learning was viewed as a checkbox rather than a valued achievement. Engagement in development programs has declined, and high performers have sought organizations where their growth would be recognized and rewarded.

Leadership win. At Company T, the leadership team has made learning recognition a core part of their culture. Managers give regular shout-outs for completed courses, feature team members in internal newsletters, and tie learning milestones to performance incentives. When a team member has earned a data analytics certification, her manager not only has celebrated her achievement but also invited her to lead a knowledge-sharing session. The gesture has boosted morale, built confidence, and motivated others to invest in their own development. Over time, learning has become a shared value and a key driver of retention and innovation.

Recognizing the Hidden Value

The list of leadership wins and missteps could go on. These illustrative moments are shared to invite reflection. How often do you, as a leader, take shortcuts—sometimes unconsciously—for yourself, your team, or your organization? It's easy to become consumed by tasks, timelines, and outputs, losing sight of the deeper purpose behind the work: the hidden value.

That's why committing to intentional learning and development—for yourself and your team—is not just important; it's essential. Learning prowess becomes truly impactful when it is shared and extended.

This idea is at the heart of Dr. Keith Keating's second book, *Hidden Value: How to Reveal the Impact of Organizational Learning* (2025). In it, he references a powerful moment involving President John F. Kennedy and a janitor at NASA. Known for his ability to connect with everyone, JFK asked the janitor what he was doing. Without hesitation, the janitor replied, "I'm helping put a man on the moon."

The point is this: beyond our titles and day-to-day responsibilities, leaders—and those who support leadership and learning—are often the hidden enablers of what is possible and truly transformative.

As Dr. Keating describes, we are all "architects of transformation," creating ripple effects across entire organizations. Leaders are responsible for helping people become who they're meant to be. And that kind of investment leaves a lasting impression—just as you still remember the leaders and organizations that invested most in your own growth and development.

PART 2

Developing Leadership Prowess

4

What Is Leadership Prowess?

Defining Leadership Prowess

To us, leadership prowess is the pursuit of excellence across multiple dimensions: leadership, motivation, drive, growth, management, and team development. It is more than just occupying a position; it is about embodying values, leading with purpose and empathy, exercising authority with humility, and maintaining an awareness of one's positionality.

When we speak of leadership prowess, we envision a leader who is both self-aware and focused on others—someone who understands the weight of their influence and uses it to inspire and cultivate the growth of those around them.

Leadership prowess, when effectively applied, serves as a catalyst for change and development of new leaders in a world desperate for more. It is a leadership style that sparks momentum and curiosity, fosters inclusion, and opens space for others to lead and explore their strengths. At its best, leadership prowess produces more leaders—not silence, fear, or stagnation in the people they manage.

Now more than ever, our world is calling for visible and intentional leadership prowess. Why? Because of the rapid shifts

69

occurring across workplaces, political systems, educational upheaval, environmental conditions, and the growing crises confronting humanity and global communities. The demands of this moment require leaders who don't just react but who rise with purpose, empathy, vision, and resolve.

We need leaders who are intentional in their response, attitude, and approach—leaders whose gentleness and humility help others feel seen, heard, and, most important, safe, secure, inspired, and motivated to face each day with renewed momentum. These are leaders who are decisive, who lead with grace and by example, who act with courage, and who remain lifelong learners. They surround themselves with mentors, trusted advisors, and coaches—aligning their purpose with their organization's mission to lead with integrity, fairness, and impact.

The truth is, many leaders around us may never change. But the fact that you are reading this book suggests that you are already leaning into a different kind of leadership—one that is conscious, courageous, and capable of shaping the future. You're not just preparing to lead. You're preparing to lead with *prowess*.

For both Marshall and me, our leadership journeys have always been rooted in humility, purpose, action, and empathy. My own leadership prowess is visible—in how I teach and support my students in the classroom. For Marshall, it's evident in the way he coaches executives with clarity and compassion. These qualities don't make us weak or ineffective—they make us approachable, safe, and aspirational. That's the essence of leadership: to lead with purpose and inspire others to do the same.

Dean Troy Eggers, dean of Columbia University's School of Professional Studies, once shared a truth that continues to shape my leadership perspective: "If you're not effective in your leadership prowess, your leadership team will abandon ship. They'll choose to work for someone else." He went on to explain that awareness of his own positionality keeps him accountable—to model the very leadership he expects from his team. That, in itself, is a living example of leadership prowess in action. This example illustrates how leadership prowess requires both accountability and humility.

Take a moment to reflect. How visible is your leadership prowess to those around you? Do you consistently demonstrate leadership prowess, or is this an area where you're still growing? What intentional actions can you take today to improve and inspire your team? Honest reflection like this ones, are the initial first step toward aligning with your path to intentional leadership—what we call *leadership prowess in action.*

Leadership Prowess in Action

To truly understand the impact and effectiveness of leadership prowess, let's reflect on how leaders exemplify it in practice— and how you can identify your strengths and areas for intentional growth.

One such leader is Indra Nooyi, former CEO of PepsiCo. Renowned for her strategic vision, people-centered approach, and humility, Nooyi elevated PepsiCo's global standing while deeply investing in the development and purpose-driven innovation of both her team and the business.

Her leadership prowess empowered others, welcomed diverse perspectives, and demonstrated that business success and personal integrity can—and should—coexist. Nooyi didn't just lead; she built a lasting legacy that continues to inspire leaders around the world.

A striking example of her leadership prowess was her habit of writing handwritten letters to the parents of her senior leadership team, expressing gratitude for raising such capable professionals. She wrote more than 400 letters each year— personally crafted and sent. This gesture, both surprising and deeply meaningful, highlighted her profound commitment to people-first leadership. By honoring the families behind her team, she strengthened their sense of purpose and reinforced their dedication—not only to her but to PepsiCo's mission. Her team felt truly seen, and their families appreciated being recognized in this way.

This tradition stemmed from Nooyi's own experience: her parents were often praised for her career successes, and witnessing their joy inspired her to bring that same recognition to the families of her senior leaders.

Remember, the purpose of leadership prowess is not to imitate a style that doesn't align with yours; it's to help you become more self-aware and others-focused. How often do you acknowledge your team for their contributions or accomplishments? Do you recognize them only when things are going well or also during challenging or hectic times?

At every monthly faculty meeting, Dean Troy Eggers would begin by expressing his gratitude for all we do for the school and our students. He never missed this moment—even when the agenda was tough and circumstances challenging. His appreciation consistently outweighed the pressures of the day, making everyone in the room feel closer to him and truly value his leadership. Every time he spoke, we all felt seen and a great sense of belonging. How you make others feel matters, too. It has to be intentional, and consistent, because it also exhibits your values and what matters most to you when you are in a room.

Feels and Reads the Room

How many times has your heart skipped a beat when a leader walked into a room—not because they said anything, but because their presence shifted the energy? Not in a comforting way, but in a way that puts you on edge, turning steady heartbeats into anxious palpitations. Their intensity doesn't inspire—it drains. It silences voices and suffocates insight.

Now think of another leader whose presence brings calm. The moment they enter, the tension lifts. You feel safe. Seen. The fears of that moment quietly begin to fade.

The older and more experienced we become, the less tolerance we have for unnecessary anxiety in professional spaces—especially when it comes from leadership. Some leaders still believe that power is best expressed through intimidation. Wrong move. Making people feel afraid is not leadership prowess; it's something else entirely.

Whether through empathy, clarity, calm, or confidence, great leaders don't just *walk* into a room—they *tune in*. They sense, read, and respond with intention. They don't overpower; they attune. This ability to read and feel the room is one of the most underappreciated, yet essential, leadership skills. It helps others feel safe, heard, and aligned—even during moments of uncertainty. That's not accidental. That's leadership prowess in action.

Dr. Kristine Billmyer is one such leader: a professor of practice, linguist, and former dean of Columbia University's School of Professional Studies. When Dr. Billmyer enters a room, there was an immediate sense of calm, confidence, and motivation. Even when she led the conversation, the way she listened—whether to ideas or disagreement—was graceful, poised, respectful, and kind. Her presence alone inspired, offering a quiet reassurance and empowerment that you could weather any storm or reach any goal.

She had a way of making everyone feel included, seen, and heard. Often, her empathy came through effortlessly—intentional, yet so natural it seemed instinctive. That's what made it so powerful. Her leadership prowess didn't just inspire—it offered motivation and quiet reassurance to everyone around her.

So we ask you: What words will others use to describe you when you walk into a room? How do you make people feel? Do they smile, look away, cringe—or disengage entirely? Are you the kind of leader who truly cares? Does anyone notice you and your efforts?

And most important, are you being intentional about it?

How we make others feel matters—not just occasionally, but every single day. It's a consistent act of intention. True leaders inspire the room; they don't lead through fear. Because fear suppresses ideas, stalls innovation, and stifles growth. It creates a culture of stagnation.

Leadership prowess does the opposite—it creates space for possibility. And even if you think fear gives you control, make no mistake: your team is silently disengaging. They're talking—about their dissatisfaction, about you—and they're planning their exit.

Leadership prowess doesn't instill fear. It inspires progress. And if you've watched a mentor or leader use fear as a tactic, know this: that's not leadership prowess in action. That's a warning sign because eventually, that leader will be left behind: isolated, surrounded by underperformance, and responsible for a trail of burned-out teams. Is that the kind of leader you want to become? Or are you ready to lead with intention, growth, and emotional intelligence?

Not Perfectionism

Too often, we're misled by the belief that great leadership must look like perfection. But let's be honest: humans aren't perfect, and chasing an unattainable standard only breeds frustration, self-doubt, and inauthenticity.

As you read and engage with this book, know this: our goal is not to shape perfect leaders, but intentional ones—leaders who are introspective, self-aware, and committed to growth.

Intentionality is not perfection. In fact, it's far more powerful. Leading with intention means showing up fully—present, thoughtful, open to learning, and grounded in purpose. That, more than flawless execution, defines leadership prowess.

Becoming intentional starts with the mirror: assess your values, virtues, strengths, and blind spots. Consider how you respond to adversity and what feedback you consistently receive. Often, we already know where we're struggling—even if no one says it out loud. But too many confuse the need for growth with a demand for perfection. It's not.

Striving for leadership prowess is about aiming for excellence and continuous self-improvement—not flawlessness. It requires gut checks, resilience, honesty, and the willingness to evolve. It's emotional. It's hard. But it's worth it.

Because the more you grow, the more your team thrives. And over time, that growth won't just change your leadership—it will transform your life.

Transformation

What does transformation look like for you? Is it internal—rooted in personal growth—or driven by your desire to serve and uplift others? Do you need a reason why to evolve into a leader who embodies leadership prowess in action?

Maybe not. Maybe you don't need to wait for the perfect reason. Just start. Just do it. Why? Because choosing to transform makes you better—not only as a leader but also as a human being. It defines your leadership, models growth, and invites those around you to rise with you.

In a powerful conversation between Simon Sinek, bestselling author and leadership thought leader who is best known for *Start with Why* (Portfolio, 2009), and Jay Shetty, a former monk turned bestselling author, podcast host, and purpose coach, Sinek defines a leader as "the person who accepts the awesome responsibility to see others around them rise. It's about caring for people."

At its core, leadership is about care—showing up for people with intention, empathy, and courage. Leadership prowess is not about authority. It's about transformation—yours first, then theirs. Now imagine this leadership scenario—and reflect on what your leadership transformation could be.

A leader at a mid-sized nonprofit was known for her brilliance, but also for her rigidity. Her team admired her intelligence, but they feared her feedback. Her standards were high, but her patience was low. Over time, morale declined. Turnover increased. And despite her talent, her results began to suffer—not because she wasn't smart, but because she resisted change in her leadership behavior toward her team.

Everything shifted after a 360-degree review revealed how her team truly felt. At first, she was defensive. Hurt. Even angry. But then she paused, reflected, and made a choice that altered her leadership path: she committed to becoming more approachable, more human, and more intentional.

She started hosting monthly listening sessions. She asked for feedback—and acted on it. She apologized when necessary. She worked with a coach. Slowly but steadily, her team not only stayed—they flourished. And so did she.

Her transformation wasn't about being perfect. It was about being present. It wasn't about lowering her standards. It was about raising her self-awareness. And that—more than anything—became the foundation of her leadership prowess.

Feedback That Fuels Growth

One of the most powerful tools in developing leadership prowess is feedback—especially the kind that comes from those you lead and work with every day.

Marshall, one of the world's foremost executive coaches and my coauthor in this journey, pioneered the stakeholder-centered coaching method. At the heart of his approach is 360-degree feedback—but not just for the sake of evaluation. This feed-forward process is designed to drive leadership transformation.

In Marshall's model, leaders ask for feedback not only from their boss but also from peers, direct reports, and even clients. Then, they do something critical: they listen without defensiveness. They thank the people who offered insights. And most important, they follow up regularly to show their commitment to change. The transformation isn't just about self-awareness; it's about demonstrated growth in the eyes of others.

This method works because it shifts the focus from perception to progress. It invites others to be part of your development and holds you accountable in real time. Stakeholders are no longer passive observers—they become partners in your leadership evolution.

As Marshall often says, "Leadership isn't about what you say—it's about what others hear." Leadership prowess, then, isn't just about having the intent to grow. It's about making your growth *visible, consistent,* and *trustworthy.*

So we ask you: Who are your stakeholders? Do you trust them? What feedback have you been avoiding?

And most important, are you willing not just to hear it, but to act on it?

The truth is, feedback can be tough. It's not always easy to take in—especially when you're a leader who genuinely cares. In fact, the more you care, the more it can sting. You may feel frustrated, even angry, particularly when you've already been working hard to grow, evolve, and strengthen your leadership prowess.

But here's the nuance: feedback isn't an indictment of your effort—it's an invitation to sharpen your impact. Even when it's uncomfortable, it's often the most powerful catalyst for growth. And that discomfort? That's where real leadership work begins. When feedback is ignored over time, a leader's impact stalls and their growth plateaus. And make no mistake—people notice, even if they don't say a word to you.

Here is an alternate example of what happens when leaders don't heed the feedback. An executive at a fast-growing tech company was brilliant, results-driven, and widely respected for her ability to deliver under pressure. But behind closed doors, her team was disengaged, overwhelmed, and reluctant to speak up.

A 360-degree feedback review revealed the core issues: her communication style was harsh, her expectations unclear, and her team felt invisible. She skimmed the report, dismissed the findings, and told her coach, "They're just not tough enough."

Months passed. Key team members left. Innovation slowed. The once-strong culture began to fray. While she continued to meet short-term goals, she failed to build a team that could grow with her. Her leadership prowess didn't falter because she lacked talent—it faltered because she refused to listen.

The lesson here? Feedback is only as powerful as your willingness to act on it. Ignoring it doesn't make it disappear; it only guarantees that the consequences will surface later, often when it's too late to course correct.

Here's the good news, most organizations already have systems in place to help leaders gather feedback, and even better, to revisit that feedback as new habits are developed. But here's where emotional intelligence becomes critical: how a leader reads the room directly affects the honesty of the feedback they'll receive.

When leaders intimidate their teams—intentionally or not—people become hesitant, even afraid, to speak up. The result? Shallow praise, filtered truth, and missed opportunities for growth.

Marshall and I have worked with executives who initially discouraged their teams from offering hard truths. Over time, we helped them shift their perspective—teaching them to treat feedback not as criticism but as a foundation for transformation. In many cases, those difficult insights became the exact pillars on which their next phase of leadership prowess was built.

So, as you consider how to request and receive feedback from your team or key stakeholders, remember this: approach with humility, lead with kindness, and clearly articulate why you're asking. When people know you're listening to grow—not just to perform—they're more likely to trust you and invest in your development. Especially when they see that their feedback doesn't just benefit you but it also helps create a better environment for them. Everyone wins when leadership gets better.

Asking for Help *Is* Leadership Prowess

When was the last time you asked for help as a leader? How did it make you feel? How would you describe that emotion? How often do you ask for help—and whom do you turn to: your own leader, your team, a mentor, or a trusted colleague?

We often associate leadership with having all the answers, being decisive, and projecting unwavering purpose. But some of the most powerful moments in leadership don't come from knowing everything—they come from admitting when you don't. Asking for help isn't a sign of weakness. It's a profound act of strength, humility, connection, and intentionality.

It signals trust in others, self-awareness of your limits, and a genuine willingness to grow. In fact, many of the greatest leadership breakthroughs don't begin with confident answers, but with the courage to ask, "Can you help me with this?"

It's not about worrying how others will perceive you; it's about seeking the best path forward, for the sake of the team and the mission.

Yes, asking for help can make us feel vulnerable. But here's the truth: vulnerability is leadership prowess.

Vulnerability in leadership is often misunderstood—or even frowned on—in many workplaces. But let's be clear: there's nothing weak about being honest with your team when you're facing a challenge. In fact, inviting them to help solve a problem is a bold act of trust and shared purpose. It might feel uncomfortable at first—but why should you carry the weight of every solution alone?

You have a team for a reason. In many cases, you've hired, coached, and invested in that team—so why not allow them to show up fully and contribute meaningfully?

Dr. Brené Brown, renowned researcher and author, puts it plainly in *Dare to Lead: Brave Work. Tough Conversations. Whole Hearts* (Random House, 2018), "Vulnerability is not winning or losing; it's having the courage to show up when you can't control the outcome." In her view, true leadership isn't about having all the answers; it's about being intentional in creating space for others to help you find them.

So, remember this: leadership prowess isn't about being the lone expert at the top; it's about being the brave connector who knows when to ask, when to listen, and when to lean in.

Achieve Your Leadership Prowess with Habits

Habits are the foundational building blocks of leadership: small, consistent, intentional actions that compound into meaningful impact and sustainable results. They shape how we show up each day and lay the groundwork for everything else in our leadership prowess journey.

In *Atomic Habits* (Avery, 2018), James Clear writes, "Habits are the compound interest of self-improvement. Every action you take is a vote for the type of person you wish to become." His insight is simple yet transformative: systems and structures matter more than one-off achievements.

When your habits align with your identity and intentions, you stop relying on willpower alone. You begin to embody your values and redefine what leadership looks like—not just for yourself, but for those around you.

Consider this example: a senior manager at a national media organization was known for being brilliant but unpredictable— quick to deliver insights, but just as quick to interrupt, dominate meetings, and dismiss opposing views. Her performance reviews were strong, but her team struggled with morale and felt undervalued. After receiving honest feedback from a coach, she committed to one decisively simple but powerful habit: pausing before responding. Each time she felt the urge to jump in, she practiced the five-second pause—and then asked, "What do you think?"

That pause changed her leadership. It seemed small, but the habit also changed everything else. Over time, she became more trusted, more collaborative, and more aware of how her presence shaped the room. That one intentional habit, practiced consistently, became a turning point in how her leadership was experienced.

Now remember, leadership prowess isn't built overnight. It's built through the habits we choose, repeat, and refine. By picking up this book, you've taken the first step toward shaping your learning mindset, starting with intentionally adjusting your habits to embody leadership prowess in action.

We have created the following list of habits to support your desire for growth in developing your leadership prowess in action. Each habit is meant to give you multiple opportunities to refine your skills and improve your leadership habits as a leader.

Achieve Your Leadership Prowess with These 11 Habits

Habit 1: Be Intentional

Leadership is not accidental. Every day, choose how you show up with clear purpose and awareness. Intentionality shapes your actions and sets the foundation for meaningful impact. Your habits are the daily votes casting the kind of leader you aspire to be. It can be as easy as pausing to listen more to your team, and/or experimenting with something else you did to correct how you lead. Use this moment to be intentional about being more clear on your purpose and self-leadership.

Habit 2: Learn to Read the Room

True leadership is rooted in empathy and awareness. Learn to sense the unspoken dynamics in your team—notice what's said, what's left unsaid, and how people feel. This human skill enables you to respond thoughtfully, create psychological safety, and foster genuine connection and collaboration.

Habit 3: Care for Others, and Let It Show

Leadership prowess grows from authentic care. When people feel genuinely seen, heard, supported, and valued, they show up more fully. Let your empathy be visible—it inspires trust, motivation, and fosters a culture where everyone can thrive. It fosters collaboration, experimentation, and forward thinking—because you create an environment where people feel less judged to perform, and they feel more like a human being on your team, someone whose flaws are cared for and not judged. You also foster the connection between growing together as a team and winning together as a team.

Habit 4: Listen More

Listening is an active practice of humility and curiosity. Seek to understand before being understood. Make space for feedback—even when it's uncomfortable—as it's the clearest path to learning and growth. Learning to listen more helps your team troubleshoot problems and identify solutions more effectively. It also builds their confidence and gives them the flexibility to surface urgent issues that could disrupt progress or compromise task completion.

Habit 5: Be Kind

Kindness in leadership is a choice that strengthens trust and collaboration. It does not mean avoiding difficult conversations but approaching them with respect and compassion. Kindness fuels resilience and innovation in your team. Kindness also shows in how you communicate with your team—during tough conversations and otherwise. When you lead with kindness, people are more likely to truly hear what you're saying; without it, your words can become just noise.

Habit 6: Make Time to Rediscover Yourself as a Leader

Leadership prowess requires ongoing self-reflection and renewal. Regularly step back to assess your growth, celebrate progress, and identify areas to stretch. This habit keeps your leadership fresh and aligned with your evolving vision. Neglecting this often leads to increased anxiety, stress, and burnout—and if you think you're managing it well, deep down, you know you're not.

Being a great leader doesn't mean constantly pushing through; it means consistently knowing when to pause, care for yourself, and reassess whether your needs have changed. Prioritize that, and you'll lead from a place of joy and fulfillment—one that naturally radiates in your workplace.

Habit 7: Set Routine Goals for Yourself as a Leader

Intentional leadership thrives on focus and consistent structure. Set clear, measurable goals that align with your values and growth priorities. These goals will guide your habits and keep you accountable to the leader you aspire to become.

If you're unsure where to begin, explore resources and platforms that highlight emerging leadership topics and styles. Identify the attributes you'd like to adopt, and set specific, actionable goals to integrate them into your daily leadership practice.

Goal setting is a powerful leadership skill—but it's not second nature to every leader. While many understand the value of setting and meeting goals, fewer apply the same discipline to their personal growth. But why not? It takes courage and clarity to know what you want, turn it into a goal, and do what it takes to achieve it. One of the greatest marks of an effective leader is the ability to consistently set, pursue, and accomplish meaningful goals. So set them—for yourself—and make it a daily leadership habit. Encourage your team to do the same. Goal setting is more than a task—it's a gift that fuels growth and reflects the uniqueness of your leadership journey and identity.

It also gives you the opportunity to recognize and celebrate your own progress, success, and accomplishments—especially if you're in an environment where praise isn't a common practice. Set goals for yourself, and celebrate when you achieve them. That's a habit worthy of your attention and intention. It builds confidence and nurtures the leader within.

Habit 8: Build Trust with Your Team

Trust is the currency of effective leadership. It begins with demonstrating reliability, transparency, and vulnerability—creating a safe environment where people feel empowered to contribute, innovate, and grow. Trust thrives in spaces where psychological safety is nurtured and where every team member knows you have their back.

True trust flows from clarity, consistency, and intentional communication. It cannot exist when only some team members feel included while others feel left out of the "circle of trust." Be deliberate in how you build trust with each individual on your team. If you find yourself struggling to trust someone, don't ignore it—create a plan to assess the root cause and take actionable steps to rebuild that trust.

Trust isn't optional when building innovative, collaborative, and resilient teams—it's essential. And as a leader, you are solely responsible for creating and sustaining that trust. It's not something others can build for you. Take the initiative to understand what's required to strengthen trust, and commit to improving your trust-building skills. The more intentional you are in this area, the more effective and connected your team will become.

Habit 9: Ask for Help When You Need It

Asking for help is not a sign of weakness—it's a mark of leadership strength. It reflects self-awareness, humility, and a commitment to collective success. Vulnerability in seeking support fosters collaboration, deepens trust, and sets the tone for a culture where others feel safe doing the same.

As a leader, you must believe that support is available—and be willing to seek it when needed. If that doesn't feel true for you, it's time to build or strengthen your support networks—whether within your team or beyond it. Everyone needs help at some point, and asking for it is essential to thriving in leadership.

Leadership is not meant to be lived in isolation. The most effective leaders create environments where help is freely given and received. If building that kind of space is a challenge for you, start by making it a habit to ask for help. Far too many leaders carry the weight of their role alone, pushing through stress and burnout in silence.

Don't let "carrying it all alone" become your legacy. Share the load when needed—and recognize those moments as powerful teaching opportunities for those you lead.

Habit 10: Be Accountable

Own your impact—fully. Embrace feedback, learn from mistakes, and model responsibility. Accountability builds credibility, strengthens trust, and inspires your team to do the same.

In Chapter 6, we introduce the leadership accountability scale, which outlines both internal and external accountability influences. Accountability is a leadership skill that some master naturally, while others find it more challenging. For some, owning their mistakes feels intuitive; for others, knowing when—and how—to accept responsibility is less clear.

Ask yourself: which kind of leader are you? And more important, how can you build a bridge to make accountability more visible in your leadership?

When leaders demonstrate accountability without fear or defensiveness, their teams thrive. Teams begin to mirror that behavior, owning their outcomes and supporting one another through challenges. As a leader, you set the tone. If you want a culture of accountability, model it consistently—and visibly. Celebrate it, talk about it, and demonstrate it in your everyday decisions.

Don't worry about how your team will perceive your accountability. This isn't about taking the blame for things outside your control. It's about owning what falls within your leadership care—your decisions, your impact, your follow-through.

Accountable leaders operate with humility and emotional intelligence. They lead not from ego, but from a place of courage, clarity, and integrity. And that's the kind of leadership others will come to admire.

Remember: failing to be accountable is leading blindly. Your team will mirror your behavior—if you avoid ownership, they will, too. But when you lead with accountability, you build a legacy of trust, respect, and high performance.

Be accountable. It matters—and it's a leadership habit worth practicing, visibly and consistently.

Habit 11: Trust Yourself

Believe in your capacity to lead, grow, and adapt. Trust your intentions and decisions while remaining open to learning and evolving. Self-trust gives you the confidence to navigate uncertainty with resilience and grace.

To continuously build trust in yourself, you must first understand when and why that trust begins to diminish. It may erode after a poor decision, when plans fall apart, or when your team isn't responding to your leadership. It may fade when your responsibilities shift and you feel uncertain or lost. Sometimes, self-trust weakens simply because you haven't nurtured it or practiced the habit of believing in yourself.

Even the most accomplished leaders experience doubt— especially when navigating unfamiliar territory or facing the fear of the unknown. The key is to stay the course. Like experienced pirates sailing through turbulent waters, successful leaders understand that moments of hesitation—freeze, fight, or flight—are part of the journey. And yet, they continue forward, because leadership demands resilience.

Pirates and workplace leaders may seem worlds apart, but they share one critical truth: both must lead others through uncertainty. Pirates face the physical dangers of the open sea; leaders in the workplace face the emotional and strategic challenges of change, pressure, and expectation. Both carry the weight of responsibility. And both must learn to trust in their self-leadership.

The more grounded you are in self-trust, the more effective you become. It sharpens your judgment in moments of uncertainty and strengthens your ability to take decisive, values-aligned action. Mastering this habit isn't just beneficial; it's essential to how you lead today and in the future.

The best part about self-trust is that it can be developed. It doesn't need to be forced—it grows naturally when you become aware of what's holding you back. That awareness helps you find the balance to manage your self-trust, both when it feels distant and when it feels strong.

Think of self-trust like a fuel tank. It's normal for it to run low at times, but it's dangerous to let it run empty. When your self-trust is low, you become more cautious, hesitant, and less able to move forward with confidence. That's why it's important to check in regularly and refuel, through reflection, action, and grace.

Make it a habit to trust yourself and do whatever it takes to never run on empty. Self-trust is yours to manage. It's often invisible to others, and there's no shame in feeling it slip away at times. What matters most is making it a habit to restore that trust—again and again.

Stepping Forward with Leadership Prowess

These 11 habits offer an ongoing framework to strengthen your leadership skills and deepen your impact. As your mindset shifts and new challenges emerge, your habits should evolve, too—that's the essence of being a lifelong learner and putting leadership prowess into practice. To help you begin, here are some real-world examples that can guide you in choosing which of these 11 habits to focus on first.

Leadership Prowess Habits Self-Assessment

The path to leadership prowess begins with honest self-awareness and a focus on others. This self-assessment is designed to help you pause, reflect, and take stock of where your current habits align—or don't—with your intentions as a leader. It's not a test; it's a tool for clarity.

As you go through each habit, your answers will help reveal which areas need more attention and which are already part of your leadership strengths. This process will support you in prioritizing the right habits at the right time, so your growth is intentional, not accidental.

Assessment Instructions

For each habit, answer the questions with a simple yes or no. Be truthful with yourself; this is an opportunity, not a performance. It wasn't designed for perfection but to increase your self-awareness and accountability.

Habit 1: Be Intentional

- Do you set a clear purpose before important meetings or decisions? (yes/no)
- Are you aware of how your daily actions align with your leadership goals? (yes/no)
- Do you consciously decide how you want to show up each day as a leader? (yes/no)

Habit 2: Learn to Read the Room

- Do you pay attention to unspoken cues like body language and tone in conversations? (yes/no)
- Can you adjust your communication style based on the mood or needs of your team? (yes/no)
- Do you notice when people seem hesitant or disengaged and respond accordingly? (yes/no)

Habit 3: Care for Others, and Let It Show

- Do you make an effort to acknowledge and celebrate your team members' contributions? (yes/no)
- Are you comfortable showing empathy openly when team members share challenges? (yes/no)
- Do you follow up to check in on people's well-being beyond just work tasks? (yes/no)

Habit 4: Listen More

- Do you listen fully without interrupting during conversations? (yes/no)
- Do you ask clarifying questions to ensure you understand others' perspectives? (yes/no)
- Are you open to feedback—even when it's critical—and use it to improve? (yes/no)

Habit 5: Be Kind

- Do you approach difficult conversations with respect and compassion? (yes/no)
- Are you mindful of your tone and words to avoid causing unnecessary stress? (yes/no)
- Do you recognize and model kindness as a core leadership value? (yes/no)

Habit 6: Make Time to Rediscover Yourself as a Leader

- Do you regularly schedule time for self-reflection on your leadership journey? (yes/no)
- Do you set aside moments to celebrate your progress and achievements? (yes/no)
- Are you open to evolving your leadership style based on new insights? (yes/no)

Habit 7: Set Routine Goals for Yourself as a Leader

- Do you create clear, measurable leadership goals? (yes/no)
- Do you review your progress on these goals regularly? (yes/no)
- Are your goals aligned with your core values and leadership vision? (yes/no)

Habit 8: Build Trust with Your Team

- Do you communicate openly and transparently with your team? (yes/no)
- Are you consistent in following through on your commitments? (yes/no)
- Do you share your vulnerabilities appropriately to create psychological safety? (yes/no)

Habit 9: Ask for Help When You Need It

- Are you comfortable admitting when you don't have all the answers? (yes/no)
- Do you actively seek support or input from others when facing challenges? (yes/no)
- Do you model asking for help as a strength to your team? (yes/no)

Habit 10: Be Accountable

- Do you own your mistakes openly and learn from them? (yes/no)
- Do you hold yourself to high standards and expect the same from others? (yes/no)
- Do you give credit to others and avoid blaming? (yes/no)

Habit 11: Trust Yourself

- Do you make decisions with confidence while being open to new information? (yes/no)
- Are you comfortable navigating uncertainty without second-guessing constantly? (yes/no)
- Do you believe in your ability to grow as a leader even when facing setbacks? (yes/no)

How to Use Your Results on Your Leadership Prowess Habits Self-Assessment

After completing the assessment, take a moment to count how many times you answered no for each habit.

Habits with two or more no responses indicate areas that need your attention and should be prioritized for growth. These are the habits in which developing your skills will have the greatest impact on your leadership prowess.

Habits in which you answered yes most of the time are strengths you can maintain. While these may require less immediate focus, continue nurturing them to sustain your progress.

Now you can get started on your leadership development journey by selecting two to three habits where you have the highest number of no answers. Focusing on these areas first will help you build momentum and create meaningful change.

Remember, leadership prowess is an ongoing journey of learning and growth. Use your results as a guide to refine your habits intentionally and become the leader you aspire to be.

For even deeper insight, invite a coach or trusted colleague to take the assessment on your behalf. Their perspective can reveal hidden strengths, surface blind spots, and highlight exactly where your next leadership breakthrough can happen.

Remember: leadership prowess isn't about being perfect; it's about being committed. Stay curious, stay intentional, and keep growing. Let your results guide you toward the leader you are becoming—one habit at a time.

As we close this chapter, remember this: strengthening your leadership prowess isn't just a professional pursuit; it's a personal transformation. When you lead with intention and align your habits with your values, you become more open to feedback, more courageous in tough conversations, more willing to be vulnerable, and more committed to learning and growing.

Choose progress over perfection. Choose habits that reflect who you truly want to become. And most important, choose to lead with excellence and empathy—every single day—for that is leadership prowess in action.

As you grow in your leadership, remember that you can maintain existing habits, discover new ones, or expand on the ones we've shared here. What matters is your awareness. There will be times when flexibility becomes the most important leadership habit, one that requires deep reflection and intentional action.

Adding to your habits does not make you weak; it's a sign of strength. It's leadership prowess in action: recognizing that growth requires evolution. Where you are today is important, but where you want to be tomorrow may call for an extension of your leadership toolkit.

As you shift roles, take on new responsibilities, or step into new organizations, be open to adapting and expanding your habits. Let the feedback from your self-assessments guide you—especially during moments of transition or growth in your career.

Habits give us balance. They create the consistency we need to lead effectively and make wise, value-driven decisions. Keep refining them. Keep growing. And keep choosing the leader you want to become.

5

Why Do Leaders Fail, and How Can You Succeed?

Our Reactions to Failure: Past Versus Future

Why is it that the word *failure* so often stirs up stress, anxiety, or shame, when in truth, it's simply part of the game? Failure is the uncomfortable, yet essential, side of growth. While it can feel like a setback, it's often an invitation: to pause, reflect, and rise stronger. When met with intention, failure becomes one of our most powerful teachers: redirecting us toward transformation, new possibilities, and greater effectiveness.

To lead with intention means understanding that failure is not always a reflection of incompetence; it can result from unforeseen variables, evolving dynamics, or bold experimentation. That's why thoughtfully assessing risk and preparing for potential failure is a sign of leadership prowess in action. Yes, setbacks in strategy, discovery, execution, or communication are inevitable—some within your control, others not. But what matters most is how you respond and what you learn from every action.

This chapter explores why leaders fail—and, more important, how you can succeed. By becoming more intentional, self-aware, and adaptive, you can reduce the likelihood and impact of failure and transform challenges into catalysts for reinvention.

Often, when we think about failure—past or future—it's not that we've actually failed yet. Instead, it's the *fear* of failure that quietly holds us back. For many new and emerging leaders, that fear becomes one of the biggest reasons they fall short— not because they couldn't succeed, but because they never fully stepped into the arena.

But what if we flipped that mindset? What if, instead of fearing failure, we studied it? What if we examined the reasons other leaders fall short—not to criticize, but to gain insight? Understanding what causes leadership failure enables us to prepare better, act smarter, and lead more boldly.

Neglecting Your Well-Being Is a Leadership Failure

More often than we care to admit, many leaders are only just beginning to prioritize their own mental health—while others still struggle to commit to even the most basic routines of self-care. Yet, the cost of neglect is staggering. Globally, poor mental health—such as depression and anxiety—contributes to over $1 trillion in lost productivity each year, according to the World Health Organization.[1] In the United States alone, organizations lose about $44 billion annually due to depression-related issues, finds the *Journal of Clinical Psychiatry*.[2]

---

[1]World Health Organization. (2017, September). Mental health in the workplace: Information sheet. WHO. https://www.who.int/publications/i/item/WHO-MSD-17.2

[2]Stewart, W. F., Ricci, J. A., Chee, E., Hahn, S. R., & Morganstein, D. (2003). Cost of lost productive work time among U.S. workers with depression. *JAMA, 289*(23), 3135–3144.

Effective leadership starts from within. Before managing others, managing outcomes, or driving innovation—ask yourself these questions:

- Are you truly taking care of yourself?
- How do you measure or track your own well-being?
- How proactive are you about your mental and emotional health?
- Do you treat it as essential, or as optional?
- What does a healthy, balanced mental state actually look like for you?

Only you can take care of yourself. Only you can prioritize your well-being; the quality of your leadership depends on it.

We live in a world where overwork is often glorified, yet there are far too many cases—some heartbreaking—where people have pushed themselves beyond the point of recovery. Workplace deaths and burnout-related illnesses are no longer isolated incidents; they are a reflection of a system in desperate need of change.

Let that change begin with you. Prioritize your mental health. Ask for help when you're struggling. Adjust your schedule to make space for rest, therapy, reflection, or any practice that nurtures your wholeness. Whether you realize it today or a month from now, every step you take toward self-care builds your resilience and strengthens your ability to lead with clarity, empathy, and purpose. The truth is when your well-being thrives, your leadership does, too.

Leadership prowess is also recognizing that caring for yourself is not optional; it's foundational. Prioritizing your personal well-being and taking corrective action is a powerful act of self-leadership.

Neglecting Your Team's Well-Being Is a Leadership Failure

There is a clear and powerful connection between a leader who intentionally manages their own well-being and one who effectively supports the well-being of their team. When a leader neglects the emotional and mental health of their people, they risk creating a high-stress, toxic work environment, one that stifles creativity, erodes trust, and accelerates burnout.

Overlooking your team's individual well-being is not just an oversight, it's a leadership failure. While it's true that leaders may not always be aware of personal challenges affecting a team member's performance, it is still your responsibility to create a culture where those challenges can be safely shared. That's what leadership prowess looks like in practice.

It begins with this question, "Do your team members feel safe enough to bring their whole selves to work?" Your ability to cultivate psychological safety—to build an environment where people feel comfortable speaking openly about challenges, both personal and professional—is what sets great leaders apart.

Yes, we live in a world where professional and personal lives are often compartmentalized. But exceptional leadership requires empathy, presence, and a genuine effort to know your people beyond their job titles. When you create space for honest conversations and respond without judgment, you model the kind of leadership that inspires others to follow—and, one day, lead like you.

In short, when you care for your team's well-being, you're not just leading a team, you're shaping future leaders.

You might be asking yourself, "If I already do this well, is there more to be done?" The answer is yes. If you are already leading with empathy and intentionality, then your next step is to teach others to do the same within their teams. The true power of leadership prowess lies not only in what you do but also in your ability to multiply that impact through others.

What sets extraordinary leaders apart is the understanding that caring for your team's well-being is not optional. It is a nonnegotiable responsibility, one that must be modeled, nurtured, and passed on. Teaching your team to lead with this same care and commitment is where the magic of sustainable, transformative leadership begins.

Why? Because when people feel genuinely valued, they show up differently. They're more committed, more loyal, and more willing to invest in the collective mission. This isn't about performance for the sake of appearances, it's about real care. It's about demonstrating a style of leadership that others want to follow and emulate.

Marshall and I are often asked why we lead with so much care. The answer is simple: because we genuinely care. We understand that the way we show up in our leadership becomes the foundation others will build from. And that's not just influence, that's legacy.

Neglecting to Seek Community Is a Leadership Failure

During the pandemic, when virtual learning became the norm, Dean Eggers created a virtual community of deans from Ivy League schools to exchange ideas and learn from each other.

The group was created to increase accessibility of information across schools and to share the responsibility of working together to support their respective universities and students—especially during a time of unprecedented challenges when collaboration was essential for survival and success.

This community has endured well beyond the pandemic, a testament to the power of partnership, relationships, and meaningful connection, and a true example of leadership prowess in action.

Leaders are not meant to operate in isolation. It's essential to find and nurture a community that supports your growth and transformation. There is tremendous value in sitting among like-minded individuals where collaboration—not competition—is the driving force.

My coauthor, Marshall, founded the Marshall Goldsmith 100 Coaches community—a vibrant, global network of executive coaches and leaders dedicated to continuous learning and mutual support. This community is built on principles of trust, accountability, and shared growth, where members openly celebrate each other's wins, challenge one another to improve, and provide honest feedback. Through regular conversations, coaching exchanges, and shared resources, the 100 Coaches group exemplifies how a supportive community can amplify leadership impact far beyond individual efforts.

So, we ask you these questions: Do you belong to a community? Do you have a professional group where you can be authentic, vulnerable about your experiences, and share your challenges? How often do you make time to reconnect or stay connected? Or has your leadership journey been a solo one?

Community is a place to lean on others and face workplace challenges alongside people who understand and support you. It can be a community of supporters or a community of practice—where knowledge and ideas flow freely, expanding your ability to lead with intention, purpose, and courage. Within such a community, you can challenge yourself to think differently, respond more effectively, and stay ahead of the curve.

To see this in action, let's look at Maya's story. Maya, a mid-level manager at a fast-growing tech company, faced sudden team burnout caused by tight deadlines and shifting priorities. Feeling overwhelmed and unsure how to best support her team, she chose not to struggle alone. Instead, she reached out to a professional leadership community she belonged to, a diverse group of leaders from various industries who met virtually each month.

Through open dialogue and shared experiences, Maya gained new strategies for promoting work-life balance, setting realistic expectations, and fostering open communication within her team. Beyond practical advice, the community provided emotional support, reminding her that leadership challenges are common and manageable with the right mindset and tools.

Empowered by this collective wisdom and encouragement, Maya returned to her team with renewed energy and actionable plans that successfully reduced burnout and improved morale. The community's ongoing support continues to nurture her growth as a more resilient and empathetic leader.

Remember, leadership thrives in community. Your ability to seek, build, and engage with others is a cornerstone of enduring success. When choosing a professional community, look for one that truly aligns with your values, goals, and personality. Without this alignment, the value you gain—and your potential to grow and thrive—can be limited.

Sometimes, a community doesn't have to be a formal group; it can be a circle of trusted colleagues or professional friends inside or outside your workplace—whichever feels most authentic and supportive to you. They will be your community, and you theirs, built on mutual trust and respect for each individual's perspective and background.

The key is to lean on your community for guidance, encouragement, and fresh perspectives. Doing so will empower you to lead differently, embrace continuous growth, and expand your leadership prowess in action.

Neglecting to Invest in Oneself Is a Leadership Failure

We've previously discussed why investing in yourself is essential. In this section, we emphasize why failing to do so is not just a missed opportunity but also a failure in leadership.

Have you ever worked in an organization where legacy employees—those who have been with the company for decades—are highly regarded for their tenure and institutional knowledge? While experience is invaluable, it should never become an excuse to stop growing. Time served is not a substitute for continuous learning.

Too often, we encounter experienced leaders who haven't pursued growth beyond what their learning and development teams offer. In such cases, these leaders might misunderstand the intent behind calling lack of investment a failure. But the truth is, if your learning has stalled, so has your leadership.

The good news is that many organizations offer development programs, training, and sponsorships to help their leaders evolve. However, when leaders recognize that their current learning experiences aren't moving the needle and choose to remain silent, that silence becomes a failure. Failing to advocate for your own growth is a missed opportunity—not just for yourself, but for your team and organization as well.

Leadership prowess in action means taking ownership of your development. It requires going beyond what is offered, being proactive, and aligning your learning with the evolving needs of your team and organization. In today's rapidly changing world, the most effective leaders are those who never stop learning.

The time for excuses is over. Whether you are tenured or newly promoted, setting aside time to reassess what you *still need* to know is a critical marker of leadership success.

It reflects a mindset that not only shapes the health and innovation of your organization but also determines whether you reach your leadership aspirations or fall short. Those who thrive invest in their learning prowess. Those who don't, often get left behind.

That said, learning without intention or purpose is just as dangerous. It becomes noise—wasted time, wasted energy. When organizations constantly face pressure to stay agile, competitive, and innovative, your personal development must also be tied to clear goals. Isn't the ultimate purpose of growth to accelerate your career and fulfill your leadership potential?

We hope your answer is the same as ours: yes.

When learning is done with clarity and conviction, results follow, even when the journey includes uncertainty or setbacks. The link between intentional learning and effective leadership is undeniable. And in the long run, it's what separates leaders who stay relevant from those who get stuck in the past.

We know that the workplace is a hybrid of brilliant backgrounds, tacit knowledge, and lived experiences. That's why we want to share two contrasting examples of how leaders are perceived: one who relies solely on tenure and one who continually invests in learning to grow their impact.

Kevin had been working at his company for over 18 years. Known for his institutional knowledge and history with the organization, Kevin was respected but not necessarily looked to for innovation. When new technologies and practices were introduced, Kevin often deferred, citing his years of experience and what had "always worked." He attended mandatory training sessions but rarely applied the new strategies to his work.

His team, while loyal, began to fall behind in performance compared to others who were more adaptive. Over time, Kevin's influence began to wane, and opportunities for advancement surpassed him, and some of his team members were promoted to roles that the organization could not rely on his efforts, which often made Kevin sad and depressed.

By contrast, Jasmine, a mid-career leader with 10 years of experience, consistently sought ways to evolve. She participated in leadership coaching, enrolled in specialized courses, and frequently invited her team to co-learn and co-lead with her.

Rather than relying solely on what she already knew, Jasmine stayed curious and open. Her team noticed—and responded. Engagement rose, innovation flourished, and Jasmine was soon tapped to lead a company-wide transformation initiative. Eventually, Jasmine was promoted to run a global team.

The difference? Jasmine chose to grow. Kevin chose to stay comfortable.

Leadership isn't a reward for the past; it's a responsibility to the future. And that future belongs to those who commit to learning—not just once, but continuously.

But let's be clear: learning isn't just for your organization or your team—it's for *you*. Embracing learning and growth is one of the most powerful ways to care for your own well-being. A learning mindset transforms uncertainty into clarity, reduces anxiety, broadens your perspective, and shapes how you lead and show up with grace, intention, purpose, and action. It's a mindset that's contagious, courageous, and deeply aspirational for your team, your peers, and yourself.

So do it for your health, too. Invest in your development not because it's expected of you but because *you're worth it*. You deserve the time, the effort, and the transformation. And the health benefits are real.

When continuous learning becomes part of your leadership DNA, the returns aren't just measurable, they're often immeasurable. A growing body of research links lifelong learning to improved health outcomes: longer lifespans, stronger emotional resilience, and notable reductions in depression, anxiety, and other health-related concerns.

In other words, investing in your growth isn't just a career advantage—it's a lifelong act of self-care. And that's a major win—not just for your leadership journey but also for your well-being, your confidence, and the way you demonstrate your leadership prowess in action.

Neglecting Company Culture Alignment Is a Leadership Failure

It is important to state here and now that some leaders struggle because the organizational culture doesn't align with their values. When there's a mismatch between personal beliefs and workplace norms, leaders become disillusioned, disengaged, or inauthentic.

This reality often leads to stagnation in their roles and even personal health challenges. As we shared in Chapter 3, quoting Peter Drucker, "Culture eats strategy for breakfast." Ignoring culture alignment only increases the risk of failure. The more your company culture aligns with your leadership, the more you will thrive. The more you ignore that alignment, the more you struggle.

We understand that, in some cases, when you first join an organization, the culture aligns well with your values. That alignment may be why you were initially drawn to the company. But over time, with leadership changes, organizational growth, or new partnerships, the culture can shift.

Even when you remain committed to the organization, if you don't work to improve or adapt the culture, you risk unraveling as a leader—something your team and colleagues will notice. This silence and inaction can diminish your reputation as leadership prowess in action.

The goal of this section isn't to suggest that you leave your current role—it's to encourage honest reflection. How well does your workplace culture align with your personal values? Are you motivated to invest your time and energy in influencing and rebuilding that culture? Or might it serve your growth better to seek new opportunities elsewhere?

The decision is yours, and it hinges on the future you envision and the limitations you may be experiencing within your current environment. As Simon Sinek notes, leaders who cannot authentically connect their values with their organization's culture face greater challenges in inspiring others and sustaining long-term success.[3]

Now, let's explore three common scenarios leaders often encounter when your values no longer align with your company's culture—and how that misalignment can either hinder your success or spark meaningful transformation.

First, there's Jordan, a senior leader at a global logistics firm. After a major acquisition, the once people-first culture he thrived in became increasingly metrics-driven and transactional.

Though Jordan remained a strong performer, the shift left him feeling disconnected, unheard in leadership meetings, and unsure of how to contribute meaningfully. Instead of voicing his concerns or seeking allies, he chose to stay silent, assuming his tenure would protect him. But over time, his influence declined, his team disengaged, and burnout quietly set in.

As his sense of purpose eroded, so did his well-being; depression and anxiety set in, affecting his leadership and his life beyond the office.

Is this you? Are you the kind of leader who stays silent during a cultural drift?

Then there's Sasha, a department head at a health care company who began to notice a shift toward competitive individualism—at odds with her collaborative leadership style. Rather than tolerate the change, Sasha took time to reflect, reconnected

---

[3]Sinek, S. (2009). *Start with why: How great leaders inspire everyone to take action.* Portfolio/Penguin.

with her professional community, and then initiated candid conversations with HR and senior leadership about what had been lost.

She proposed a path forward to revive the company's foundational values of empathy and teamwork. Through cross-functional workshops and a new mentorship program, she helped rebuild the culture she believed in. Her efforts didn't just preserve her influence—they elevated her reputation as a courageous, values-driven leader.

Do you identify more with Sasha's approach? Are you the kind of leader who chooses to act? And, are you well equipped to take action?

If so, start by reconnecting with your professional community: seek guidance, explore options, and develop a plan. Changing culture isn't a solo mission, but with allies and intention, your leadership can drive meaningful impact.

Finally, there's Malik, a seasoned tech executive who once thrived at a fast-growing startup known for its transparency and innovation. As the company scaled and investor pressure intensified, the culture shifted toward fear-based decision-making and aggressive growth-at-all-costs. Malik tried to adapt, but the gap between his values and the company's practices widened.

After months of reflection, he made the decision to leave. He later joined a B Corp that aligned with his commitment to ethical growth—and his leadership flourished. His decision to leave became the most liberating and strategic choices of his career.

Or do you identify with Malik's path? Are you the kind of leader who chooses to leave?

Either way, honor your choice without judgment. Walking away isn't failure; it's a powerful act of self-leadership. When misalignment affects your performance, your presence, and your well-being, the cost of staying often outweighs the risk of change. And if you're wondering what would happen to Malik's team—the truth is, we don't always know.

But this we do know: the company will move on. They will hire a new leader or promote from within. And that leader will have their own decisions to make—just as Malik did, and you may need to someday.

These three scenarios reflect a simple truth: leadership prowess isn't just about what you achieve; it's about how well your environment supports who you are. When your values and company culture are out of sync, you face a choice: stay silent, speak up, or move on. Just don't ignore the dissonance. The cost of inaction is your energy, your effectiveness, your well-being, your success, and more important, your continued joy as a leader.

Proactive Leadership: The Path to Lasting Success

Here's what's fascinating: sometimes failure is a tangible reality, and other times it's a matter of mindset. To help you refocus and better distinguish between failure as reality versus the perception of failure, use the following assessment to check in with yourself and your self-leadership.

Self-Leadership Mindset Assessment

Similar to the type of assessment in Chapter 4, this assessment is a self-leadership mindset assessment. The questions are designed to help you reflect on how you handle similar workplace situations and to ensure you are currently in a space that supports your thriving, your success, and your leadership prowess in action.

Assessment Instructions

For each question, answer with a simple yes or no. Be honest with yourself—this is a personal check-in, not a performance review. This assessment isn't about perfection; it's designed to help you strengthen your self-leadership and increase your awareness of where you stand.

Our Reactions to Failure: Past Versus Present

- Do you view failure as an opportunity for growth rather than a reflection of your worth? (yes or no)
- When faced with setbacks, do you consciously adjust your mindset instead of dwelling on past mistakes? (yes or no)
- Are you able to separate past failures from your current leadership potential? (yes or no)

Neglecting Your Well-Being Is a Leadership Failure

- Do you regularly prioritize your mental and physical well-being alongside your leadership responsibilities? (yes or no)
- Have you noticed any negative impact on your health due to work stress or leadership challenges? (yes or no)
- Do you take proactive steps to manage stress and prevent burnout? (yes or no)

Neglecting Your Team's Well-Being Is a Leadership Failure

- Do you actively check in with your team's emotional and professional well-being? (yes or no)
- Are you aware of signs of disengagement or burnout within your team? (yes or no)
- Do you foster a work environment that supports your team's health and growth? (yes or no)

Neglecting to Seek Community Is a Leadership Failure

- Do you have a professional community or network you can turn to for support and advice? (yes or no)
- When facing challenges, do you seek feedback and perspectives from trusted colleagues? (yes or no)
- Are you open to collaborating and sharing experiences with other leaders to grow? (yes or no)

Neglecting to Invest in Oneself Is a Leadership Failure

- Do you commit time regularly to learning and personal development? (yes or no)
- Have you reflected on how continuous learning affects both your leadership and well-being? (yes or no)
- Do you invest in skills or experiences that align with your values and career goals? (yes or no)

Neglecting Company Culture Alignment Is a Leadership Failure

- Do you feel that your personal values align with your organization's culture?(yes or no)
- Have you taken steps to address any cultural misalignments that affect your leadership effectiveness? (yes or no)
- If misalignment persists, have you considered what actions you might take to protect your well-being and leadership impact? (yes or no)

How to Use Your Results on Your Self-Leadership Mindset Assessment

After completing the assessment, take a moment to count how many times you answered no and how many times you answered yes. Areas where you have two or more no responses indicate mindsets that need your attention and should be prioritized for clarity and growth. Improving these areas will have the greatest impact on your leadership prowess.

Responses where you answered yes most of the time represent strengths you can maintain. While they may require less immediate focus, continue nurturing these strengths to sustain your progress.

Once you've reviewed your results, start your self-leadership journey by selecting two to three habits with the highest number of no answers. Focusing on these areas first will help you build momentum and create meaningful change.

Remember to review your responses with a professional licensed coach, a trusted mentor, or a supportive colleague who can offer guidance. This is not the time to sit in isolation but an opportunity to reinvent yourself and your leadership prowess. Seek the support and improve your leadership skills.

Leading Through Reflection: When It Matters Most

If transformation is your goal, you must identify meaningful ways to support your growth and deepen your resilience and grit. Seek out practical strategies to strengthen your leadership capacity. When imbalance persists, the consequences are real—stress and anxiety can quietly erode your effectiveness.

Often, leaders remain unaware of this weight or choose to ignore it, brushing it off and jumping back into action and hoping that momentum alone will change the circumstances. But denial rarely leads to meaningful change.

Every leader strives for success. Every aspiring leader longs for the opportunity to lead. Yet every leadership role comes with its own challenges, roadblocks, and responsibilities.

The famous phrase "Uneasy lies the head that wears the crown" comes to mind. No one said it would be easy, but it isn't always difficult either. Leadership can be exciting, joyful, adventurous, rewarding—even magical—when everything aligns. But true leadership is revealed in the moments when it doesn't.

Leadership is a reflection of your values and priorities. It's always on display: through your actions, your decisions, and how you show up in difficult moments.

You have a choice: to check in with yourself or to look the other way. This is why self-leadership is essential to your success. When you consistently check in with yourself, you create the conditions for healthier teams, meaningful mindset shifts, and deeper engagement across your organization.

If culture and community are important to you as a leader, seek alignment with organizations that reflect those same values. When your personal values match the values of your workplace, you create the conditions to grow and thrive within the organization.

Leading multiple teams and staying agile requires not only strategic thinking but also a supportive environment that fuels your energy and ambition. Let the energy of that space empower you to reach new levels of success and build cross-functional teams that collaborate, support one another, and drive collective achievement.

6

How Can You Leverage Leadership Accountability?

Accountability Is Leadership Prowess in Action

Accountability is more than a leadership buzzword—it's a sign of intention. Being accountable means choosing to lead with clarity, consistency, and purpose. It is a reflection of leadership prowess and a deliberate decision to prioritize personal growth, self-discovery, team trust, and sustainable impact.

While most leaders understand the *importance* of accountability, many struggle when it comes to applying it in practice. Often, they rely solely on personal accountability, believing their inner drive is enough. But true leadership accountability requires more—it demands a balanced approach that includes both internal and external influences.

Two of our favorite executive coaches and friends, Scott Osman and Jacquelyn Lane, teamed up with Marshall Goldsmith to write the book, *Becoming Coachable*, a powerful exploration of what it means to open yourself to growth. The book sheds light on the nuanced dynamics leaders face when embracing coaching, including the deeper, sometimes metaphysical, motivations behind that decision.

113

One of the key takeaways from their brilliant work is this: personal motivation alone is rarely enough to sustain meaningful growth. While internal personal drive is essential, it often falls short when leaders are striving for continuous development or seeking to embody leadership prowess in action.

To address this gap, we developed the *leadership accountability scale*—a framework designed to help leaders recognize and intentionally strengthen both their internal and external sources of accountability. This model provides a holistic view of what it takes to sustain meaningful progress and transformation, and what it truly means to lead with accountability. The influences we highlight are based on consistent patterns we've observed in successful leaders. While we encourage you to adopt and adapt these insights, we also urge you to reflect on what balance of influences matters most to you. Let Figure 6.1 serves as a source of inspiration for creating your own personalized scale of accountability.

As seen in Figure 6.1, the key is to keep the scale balanced. While possible, what keeps our leadership accountability scale steady is the ability to identify the sources of our influence, who

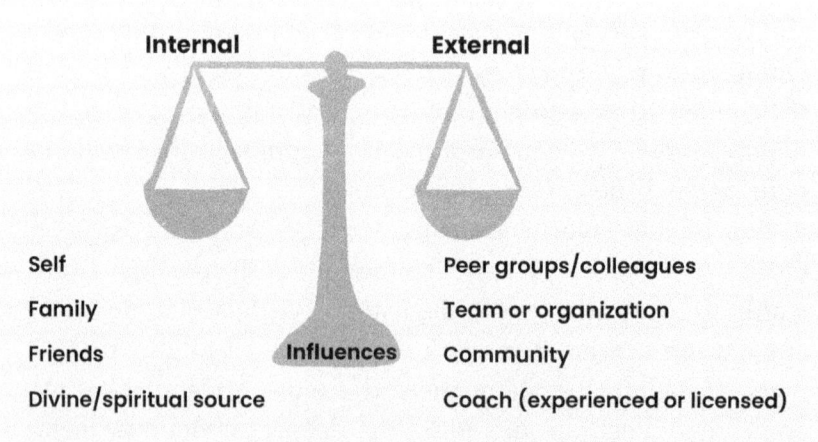

FIGURE 6.1 The leadership accountability scale.

they are, what significance do they hold, and when do we turn to them for feedback.

The leadership accountability scale is divided into two parts: internal influences and external influences. The internal sources of accountability are self (you), family, friends, and spiritual. These are self-driven or spiritually grounded forces that guide your leadership values and personal standards.

- **Self.** Your inner motivation, purpose, and drive
- **Family.** Loved ones who model integrity or hold you to your values
- **Friends.** Trusted confidants who challenge and encourage you
- **Divine/spiritual source.** Faith-based accountability or a higher calling

External sources of accountability include peer groups or trusted colleagues, community, your team and/or organization, and a coach (experienced or licensed). These are social, professional, and structural supports that provide consistent feedback, challenge your thinking, and reinforce growth through accountability.

- **Trusted colleagues/peer groups.** Fellow leaders who offer perspective, honest feedback, and opportunities for knowledge exchange
- **Community.** Networks or groups that witness your journey, offer support, and engage in the mutual exchange of insights and shared experiences
- **Team or organization.** Your formal role within a larger system that relies on your leadership and holds you accountable for both your actions and your outcomes
- **Coach (experienced or licensed).** A trained professional who serves as a trusted advisor, guiding you through intentional growth and development, helping to deepen self-awareness and facilitate transformation

Exploring the significance of both internal and external sources of accountability is essential. Doing so enables you to redefine your leadership identity, deepen your leadership prowess, rediscover your authentic self, and expand the reach of your goals and aspirations.

The First Side of Accountability: Your Internal Influences

As human beings, we navigate life through a structure and balance we hold, seek, and maintain for the sake of our existence and to regulate our sense of happiness and belonging. This state of equilibrium is shaped by our internal influences: the self, our family, our friendships, and our relationship with the divine. These core dimensions form the foundation of how we experience the world, and ultimately how we show up as accountable leaders.

Leadership Accountability Is Personal

The fragility of leadership accountability—and the balance it requires between internal and external sources—calls for a deeper examination of each side. To understand what sustains real growth, we must begin with the most important truth: it's personal.

Leadership accountability must start with you, because you are the one who drives the outcomes you want to see in yourself, your team, and your organization. You are accountable for how you lead, how you show up for others, how you create and contribute value, and how you interpret the actions and intentions of those around you. You are also responsible for aligning values, guiding your team, and stewarding the quality of what they produce.

So we ask you these questions:

- Do you feel accountable? Is it personal for you?
- Who do you feel accountable to?
- What happens when you fall short? How do you rebound?

Most successful leaders are consumed by these questions and approach their internal conflicts head-on. That's why "How do you rebound?" is part of our framework—it signals that accountability doesn't stop with failure; it begins there, within.

Family Matters

Leadership accountability starts with intentional action that begins with you, then flows outward to your kin, your colleagues, and your organization.

Former IBM CEO Ginni Rometty shared a powerful story in her memoir *Good Power: Leading Positive Change in Our Lives, Work, and World* (Harvard Business Review Press, 2023) that occurred during her Northwestern University commencement speech. In her speech, she described a moment early in her career, when she was offered a promotion, but she hesitated, unsure if she was ready.

That evening, she told her husband what had happened. His response shifted her mindset, and she returned to work the next day and accepted the promotion.

One of the key lessons she took from that experience was that growth and comfort do not coexist—a reminder that readiness doesn't always arrive before opportunity. The real growth comes in how you respond.

The takeaway from her story? Family can play a vital role in holding us accountable—to who we are, who we aspire to become, and how we show up in the world. They remind us of our worth when we question it and challenge us to take the next step toward growth and leadership.

But when family isn't present—or when your needs extend beyond their reach—accountability doesn't disappear. It evolves. Often, it transforms into the deep trust and truth-telling found in close friendships.

When Trusted Friends Become Your Accountable Partners

Sometimes, our accountability circle extends beyond blood relatives or spouses. Trusted friends, mentors, and chosen family can serve as powerful mirrors—reflecting back our values, calling us out when we're off course, and encouraging us to rise when we falter.

We recognize that not everyone has access to a supportive family system, and the world doesn't always afford the ideal. In these moments, trusted friends often step in to serve that grounding, clarifying, and motivating role.

When you read many of Marshall's books, you'll notice intentional references to his trusted friend, Mark Thompson: a respected advisor and the number one CEO executive coach. Their friendship includes daily check-ins, often multiple times a day. Mark has shared that this connection has helped him stay grounded, accountable, and ultimately, a better leader to others.

I've been fortunate to choose friends I can confide in about both personal and professional challenges. It's essential to surround yourself with people who offer wise, honest, and unbiased counsel.

For me, those people include Dr. KimLoan Tran and Dr. Keith Keating—respected chief learning officers and top industry leaders, both deeply committed to advancing human potential. They are part of my strong and small circle of trusted friends—those who hold me accountable, support my growth, and reflect the values I strive to live by.

Choose friends who align with your values and reflect the kind of leader—and person—you aspire to be. These are the people who will hold you accountable, not in an overbearing way, but with support, love, and a deep belief in your potential. They keep me grounded across all areas of life, including the personal goals I've entrusted to them.

It truly takes a village to stay accountable. And for many, that village extends beyond family and friendship. It includes a deeper connection to something greater: a source of strength, clarity, and purpose that can't always be seen but is often deeply felt.

Leadership Accountability Is Spiritual

For many leaders, accountability is deeply rooted in their spiritual beliefs. Whether expressed through religion, faith practices, meditation, or quiet reflection, this kind of grounding offers a deep sense of direction and discipline. It reinforces who you are, why you lead, and the values you bring into every decision. Spiritual accountability is often private—but its impact is profoundly public. It shapes how we lead with integrity, humility, and courage.

When Marshall Goldsmith decided to launch 100 Coaches, the timing coincided with the onset of the pandemic. He admits that, for a moment, he panicked—how would he ensure the safety and well-being of his group in such an uncertain time? In his book *The Earned Life*, he writes:

I felt as if Buddha was testing me, saying, "Okay, dude. You wanted a legacy project? This is your family now. You're going to have to earn your legacy every day by protecting it." All I had was a sense of responsibility to 100 Coaches and a renewed sense of purpose to protect it.

Marshall's spiritual reference underscores how value alignment becomes a form of daily accountability. Though personal and often unseen, our spirituality reveals itself in how we see the world, engage with others, and make decisions.

Practicing our faith can keep us humble, grounded, and focused—not driven by ambition alone, but by presence, purpose, and peace. It's a reminder that we are responsible for our efforts, not just our outcomes.

For me, my own leadership accountability is deeply rooted in my faith in God, the way I practice that faith, and the timeless teachings of the Bible. I am by no means a perfect leader—but the Bible reminds us that God's love meets us in our imperfections.

What matters most is the intention of our hearts. That belief keeps me balanced and gives me the clarity to lead, grow, and strive to be a better human and a better leader.

The Bible is filled with examples of both strong and failed leadership, offering lessons in wisdom and humility. In Proverbs Chapter 1 verse 7, you find "The fear of the Lord is the beginning of knowledge; but fools despise wisdom and instruction." These verses reflect how spiritual accountability begins with reverence, deepens through wisdom, and is ultimately revealed in how we lead others.

Spiritual accountability often goes unnoticed, yet it is more prevalent than we may realize. At some restaurants or spa locations, you'll find symbols of the owners' religious beliefs—perhaps a small shrine, a scripture plaque, or an image of a spiritual figure—offered quietly but intentionally as a sign of devotion. In professional settings, you might notice a crucifix necklace worn by a doctor, or a subtle bracelet symbolizing prayer or protection.

These outward expressions may seem small, but they often carry deep meaning. For the observer, they can evoke a quiet sense of peace—or a sense of the individual's inner compass and spiritual accountability.

Whether we fully understand the symbolism or not, we often respond with a kind of respect, recognizing that these gestures reflect a personal belief system guiding someone's actions, values, and sense of responsibility—even in public spaces beyond the walls of home or sanctuary.

So we ask you these questions:

- Is there a spiritual side to you and your leadership? How much does your belief system influence your leadership decisions and actions?
- How often do you intentionally nurture your faith or spiritual practice? Is it visible?

Remember, the focus of this part of the book is intentionality: how to lead with purpose, self-awareness, and clarity. If practicing your faith or nurturing your spiritual side is part of being your authentic self, be intentional about it. Do it consistently and meaningfully.

Internal influences exist to offer a framework for deeper insight and self-discovery. They help us create more sources of guidance, strength, and reflection. Take the time to find what grounds you. Practice your faith—or your form of spiritual alignment—in a way that supports your leadership intention, holds you accountable, and exemplifies your leadership prowess in action.

The Other Side of Accountability: Your External Influences

As we shift to the other side of the leadership accountability scale, we turn our attention to external influences: trusted colleagues or peer groups, community, your team or organization, and a coach (experienced or licensed). These are the people and structures who surround you, challenge you, and support your continued growth as a leader.

The Power of Trusted Colleagues and Peer Groups

Never underestimate the power of trusted colleagues or peer groups. For many successful leaders, accountability is reinforced through a strong network—often referred to as an *accountability group*. These are fellow leaders who provide perspective, honest feedback, and valuable opportunities for knowledge exchange.

For example, in Marshall Goldsmith's 100 Coaches community, these networks are called *connect groups*. By simply indicating your preferred meeting time, you're placed in a peer group with others from around the world who share your availability.

Each member is encouraged to present their "big five" weekly: key goals or updates that reflect personal or professional progress. These sessions create space for reflection, insight, and accountability that transcends geography and brings leaders together through shared intention and structure.

A connect group leader was assigned, and everyone had the opportunity to present. Each big five presentation had its highs and lows—some moved us to tears, while others left us feeling uplifted and optimistic.

In the end, what emerged was a deeper clarity, a refined sense of purpose, and new direction. Many of us sought thoughtful feedback and even welcomed constructive critique.

What made the experience even more powerful was that our connect group existed outside of our usual peer networks. This created a sense of newness—an opportunity to build fresh, meaningful relationships and expand our circles of influence.

The feedback and support we received weren't fleeting; they became lasting. And that kind of belief in you—from people who barely knew you but saw your potential—fueled a renewed sense of accountability. You kept going, not just for yourself, but because they believed in you, too.

Your Community Is a Place for Accountability

Some of the most successful and intentional leaders seek out communities and associations that reinforce their purpose and hold them accountable. For me, joining the Harvard Club of New York City became a powerful source of inspiration. The experience helped spark the vision for the nonprofit I later founded called the Global Connections for Women Foundation (GC4W).

GC4W is an award-winning global organization created to support women entrepreneurs and women in the workplace. Our mission is to connect, educate, and empower.

Today, the organization reaches over 500,000 people worldwide through online resources, webinars, social media engagements, and training programs. GC4W is globally recognized for its commitment to advancing equality, leadership, and entrepreneurship. Our online resources and events are open to everyone.

Whether you are part of a community or the founder of one, there is something profoundly powerful about having a space for open expression, meaningful exchange, and shared inspiration. If I hadn't joined the Harvard Club, I'm not sure I would have ever been inspired to start GC4W.

When I shared my vision with my network at the Harvard Club, their early encouragement and support gave me the confidence to move forward. As the organization began to grow, the club also served as a space where I connected with partners, donors, and supporters.

As a scholar practitioner, my mission at the Harvard Club feels different now that my personal goals and mission have transformed. Being a member of the Harvard Club inspires me to lead differently, teach differently, and contribute differently. The brilliant guest speakers, workshops, and professional development opportunities all leave a profound impact—helping me transfer learning directly into my daily practice. Every moment there shapes my sense of self—as a leader, mother, professional, educator, and human.

Community is designed to help you explore your potential, elevate your leadership, hold you accountable to your goals, and expand your professional network. It's also a place to learn from others—those who share your passions, pursuits, sense of purpose, and even your curiosity.

Lean on Your Team and Organization for Leadership Accountability

When it comes to leadership accountability in the workplace, one of the most valuable sources of support is your team and your organization. Dean Eggers once shared that a significant part of his accountability as a leader was shaped—and continually strengthened—by the relationships he built with his senior leadership team and the broader school community.

Their trust, collaboration, and expectations didn't just support him; they anchored his commitment to lead with purpose, clarity, and a deep sense of responsibility.

When a leader feels supported in this way, trust is reinforced, and their level of commitment rises. The result is a series of shared wins that foster unity, motivation, and a collective belief that success is possible—together.

Dean Eggers emphasized that his sense of duty and accountability extends beyond his leadership table, reaching faculty, students, and staff alike. When leadership accountability is influenced by strong organizational ties, leaders naturally hold themselves to a higher standard. They know they can seek support when needed—and, in turn, become a source of support for others.

This mutual sense of purpose is a cornerstone of innovative, loyal teams—teams that see their leader not as a distant figure, but as a human being navigating the complex and often unpredictable space of leadership. In many ways, the strength of a leader's accountability is reflected in the depth of support they receive.

For some of you, exploring the leadership accountability scale of both internal and external influences may have triggered a personal reflection. You might be asking yourself how these forces have shaped your own leadership, and whether you've fully recognized or leveraged their impact. For others, this reflection may reaffirm what you already practice: intentionally drawing from these influences to strengthen your leadership prowess.

Coachability: The Final Part of Leadership Accountability Scale

One of the most transformative elements of leadership accountability is coachability. At its core, coachability is the willingness to grow, adapt, and be guided by the insight of an experienced or licensed coach. It requires humility, self-awareness, and a deep commitment to continuous improvement. When embraced fully, it becomes a defining trait of truly impactful leaders.

The book *Being Coachable* By Scott Osman, Jacquelyn Lane, and Marshall Goldsmith (100 Coaches Publishing, 2023) challenges many of the misconceptions about coaching, particularly the outdated notion that seeking a coach is a sign of inadequacy.

Some leaders still hesitate to admit they're working with a coach, often out of fear that it makes them appear weak or unqualified. But the truth is just the opposite. In today's fast-moving, high-stakes environments, where leaders face both familiar and unfamiliar challenges, choosing to work with a coach is a mark of strength, not shame.

Proactively seeking the guidance of a coach signals thought leadership, foresight, and maturity. Your superiors recognize it as a sign of initiative. Your team sees you as an inspiration: someone who leads with intention and models what it means to keep growing.

When you ask Marshall what makes great leaders successful, he'll tell you that they work with a coach. He often draws a powerful parallel to elite athletes. Yes, the players win the games—but it's the coach who ensures they're ready, refined, and relentlessly focused.

When Curtis Martin, former NFL athlete and 2012 Hall of Fame inductee, was asked what he missed most about life in the NFL, his answer wasn't the fame or the competition—it was the coaching. The daily presence of someone wholly committed to your growth, holding you accountable, and challenging you to rise above your own expectations is irreplaceable.

Working with a coach offers more than just professional feedback—it becomes a personal mirror. It helps you reflect on who you are as a leader, whom you aspire to become, and how you're truly coping with the demands of leadership. Coaching creates space to pause and evaluate your leadership prowess, uncover blind spots, build new habits, and surface meaningful insights in a safe, open environment.

The right coach will support you through transitions, hold you accountable with empathy, and challenge you to think more deeply and act more intentionally. When that alignment is right, the impact becomes undeniable: your performance improves, your team thrives, and your organization strengthens in ways that are both measurable and deeply felt. It's no surprise that more organizations are expanding their leadership development resources to include coaching as a critical component.

Balancing the Scales: The Price of Leadership Prowess

Balancing our internal and external influences on the leadership accountability scale strengthens our ability to lead with both intention and purpose. But purposeful leadership doesn't happen by accident—it must be practiced.

It requires the development of habits that reflect the kind of leader we aspire to become. The more intentional we are in building those habits, the more naturally our actions align with our values—and the more powerfully we can begin to lead from within.

The price of leadership is consistency: being unwavering in how we lead, honest in how we reflect, and thoughtful in how we show up. Leadership is not for the faint of heart—it is for those willing to rise each day with renewed purpose and a commitment to do better. Leadership is visible, and it is contagious. When a leader is good, we feel it. And when they're not, we feel that, too.

The following list of habits serves as a daily reminder of what it means to lead with accountability. Consider how you might incorporate the leadership accountability scale into your own life: who will you draw into each influence group and where will you begin?

Habit 1: Daily Self Check-In

Internal influences shape how you respond to external ones. When you make space to reconnect with yourself, you strengthen your ability to lead with intention and clarity.

Build a habit of daily self-reflection. This can take many forms: journaling, meditating, reading a devotional, exercising, prayer, or simply sitting in silence. The key is to carve out private, uninterrupted time that belongs solely to you. Resist the urge to fill this space with tasks or distracting thoughts. Instead, treat it as a sacred pause, an opportunity to realign your thoughts, emotions, and energy.

Schedule this time on your calendar as a nonnegotiable appointment with yourself. If you live with others, let them know this time matters. Whether it's 15 minutes or longer, giving yourself full permission to be your focus renews your energy, strengthens your well-being, and grounds your leadership in purpose.

Decide early how much time you need and what time of day works best for you. Some prefer early mornings, others opt for late evenings or quiet weekend mornings. The timing is yours—but once you decide, stick with it. Habits are built through consistency.

At the end of each routine, take a moment to reflect:

- How do you feel at this moment?
- What do you need?
- What needs to shift in your daily rhythm?
- Who can you lean on for support?

These simple questions reinforce your self-awareness and enable the habit to evolve as you do.

Be intentional about how you protect this time—and honor it. The more consistently you check in with yourself, the more clearly and powerfully you'll show up for others.

Habit 2: Identify an Accountability Partner in a Family Member

Family can be one of the most powerful sources of internal accountability, but not every family member is the right fit for this role. Choose with care. If no one in your immediate family feels appropriate, consider a relative who shares your mindset and values.

Look for someone who does the following:

- Understands who you are and what matters to you
- Wants to see you grow and succeed
- Offers honest, compassionate feedback
- Models the kind of intentional leadership you aspire to (even if they're not on the same path)

Once you've identified the right person, initiate a conversation. Share your goals, your hopes, and the kind of support you need—whether it's encouragement, perspective, or simply a space to process. Invite them to meet with you regularly (weekly, monthly, or at key checkpoints), and clearly define what accountability will look like between you.

This habit is not about proximity—it's about trust, intention, and mutual respect. Choose wisely. Communicate openly. And embrace the powerful reflection that comes from being held accountable by someone who knows you well and believes in who you're becoming.

Habit 3: Engage a Trusted Friend as an Accountability Partner

Many of us have close friendships, but not all friendships are accountability relationships. Identify one or two friends who share your values, drive, and desire to grow. These are the relationships with the potential to support intentional leadership.

Be thoughtful in how you approach them. Don't present it casually; explain your vision. Let them know why you chose them, what this means to you, and what kind of partnership you're proposing. If you're open to a two-way exchange, say so. Some may accept, others may not, and that's okay. This habit only works when both people are invested.

Choose someone who is the following:

- Emotionally mature
- Consistent and responsible
- Willing to engage with seriousness and care
- Available to connect regularly

Once the partnership is confirmed, co-create a schedule that works for both of you. These touchpoints could include goal updates, reflection prompts, or honest and confidential check-ins. A strong accountability friendship brings perspective, encouragement, and challenge—all grounded in trust, mutual respect, and shared intention.

Remember to set clear boundaries and establish what's nonnegotiable from the start. Let your friend know that you value confidentiality in your check-ins and conversations. When expectations are clearly communicated, a friendship-based accountability partner is better equipped to navigate the significance of the role—and more likely to contribute to meaningful outcomes.

One of the best parts of creating an accountability partnership within a friendship is how it strengthens the bond. When both of you are committed to each other's growth, your connection deepens, your trust grows, and your friendship thrives.

Habit 4: Finding a Spiritual Accountability Partner

If a spiritual practice is part of your identity—or if you're seeking to explore that path—consider adding a spiritual accountability partner to your leadership journey. This habit isn't required of all leaders, but for those whose values align with faith, reflection, or a higher calling, it can be a powerful and grounding source of internal accountability.

The key here is intentionality. Choose a spiritual partner not out of obligation or expectation, but because it genuinely aligns with who you are and how you want to grow. This might be a mentor from your faith community, a friend who shares your beliefs and practices regularly, or a spiritual leader you respect and trust. For some, it may begin as simply as downloading a faith-based app or resource that offers daily devotionals—small, consistent steps that help foster deeper connection and an active faith practice over time.

If you're new to this path, take your time. Seek guidance from someone with experience—perhaps a spiritual director, a religious leader, or a close friend who is grounded in their own faith practice. Your conversations can focus on purpose, integrity, alignment, personal desires, and how your leadership might reflect your beliefs in action.

Spiritual accountability isn't about perfection—it's about presence, purpose, and intentional productivity. It's about staying rooted in something greater than yourself and being gently reminded of the values that matter most. This kind of partnership can guide and inform your leadership through faith teachings, spiritual practices, and supportive community.

When you're ready, take intentional steps to build this into your routine. Make it a habit to attend, subscribe, or listen regularly—whether it's a service, study group, podcast, or personal reflection practice. If you're someone who thrives on structure, feel free to schedule it. Choose a time, day, or space that feels comfortable and aligned with your spirit, your aspirations, and your leadership values.

Habit 5: Peer Group as Accountability Partner

Similar to the trusted friend model, developing a peer account-ability partnership requires intentionality and discernment. As the saying goes, "the blind can't lead the blind." You'll want to partner with individuals who are not only supportive but also equipped with the insight, experience, and growth mindset to help you lead more effectively.

Start by deciding whether your accountability partner should come from within your workplace or from an external professional network. Then, define a clear set of criteria. What qualities matter most to you? What kind of support do you need? How might their strengths complement your own? Consider their leadership track record, the growth they've demonstrated, and—most important—their alignment with your values, integrity, respect, positivity, and growth.

Confidentiality and honest feedback are nonnegotiables. A strong peer partner should challenge you thoughtfully, believe in your growth, and create space for open, reflective dialogue.

If you've already built trust with a colleague—someone you've had meaningful conversations with, who champions your leadership—explore whether they might be the right fit. Just make sure your leadership paths aren't in direct competition. Even the most well-intentioned relationships can become strained if your career goals begin to overlap. Alignment—not rivalry—is what makes this partnership work.

When you've identified the right person, approach them with clarity. Invite them into this mutually beneficial relationship by sharing what you need, why you value their insight, and how you see the partnership taking shape. If they agree, formalize the structure: set goals, schedule regular check-ins, and use calendar reminders to maintain momentum and consistency.

Remember, your accountability partner doesn't need to be someone at your workplace. In fact, an external peer can offer fresh perspective and distance from your day-to-day context. That said, workplace partners can be highly effective—if there's trust.

And finally, if the partnership no longer serves either of you, it's okay to part ways. Do so with gratitude. Let your partner know how much you've appreciated their time, insights, and commitment to your journey.

Habit 6: Aligning with a Professional Community for Accountability

As esteemed leaders of organizations large and small, aligning with a professional community is one of the most effective ways to stay accountable, inspired, and supported. Whether formal or informal, these communities create environments where you're surrounded by like-minded professionals who share your values, leadership prowess, ambitions, and drive for growth.

It's no surprise that many executives find connection on the golf course or through membership-based clubs. These settings naturally foster conversation, relationship building, and idea exchange in a relaxed yet purposeful way.

Take the example of comedian and producer Cedric the Entertainer, who describes his best friend, award-winning actor Anthony Anderson, as someone whose relationship with him deepened over several rounds of golf. What started as casual meetups evolved into a strong bond—and today, they're business partners and cofounders of AC Barbeque, a restaurant and seasoning brand built on friendship, shared values, a passion for good food, and mutual accountability.

Professional communities—whether industry-specific, interest-based, or lifestyle-oriented—offer a powerful form of accountability through conversation, collaboration, and proximity to people who both challenge and inspire you.

The good news for leaders is that there are many prestigious leadership and professional organizations to choose from. Your responsibility is to research and explore the ones that align with your personal values, professional goals, and long-term aspirations. Once you've identified the right fit, take the next step: join, show up, and commit to being an active participant.

When you attend events or gatherings, come prepared to learn, engage, and contribute. Be intentional in your interactions—listen actively, share thoughtfully, and follow up when connections are made. Make it a habit to participate fully. What may seem like a casual encounter could be the catalyst for new opportunities, deeper insight, or renewed leadership growth. The key is to treat every moment as a chance to further your leadership prowess and expand your influence.

Habit 7: Build a Culture of Mutual Accountability

The most successful leaders don't lead in isolation; they rely on their teams for accountability, feedback, and mutual growth. They listen, respond, and are willing to unlearn habits that no longer serve the collective mission. When it comes to establishing a culture of team accountability within your organization, the habit begins with intention—and it must be modeled from day one.

Leadership isn't about perfection; it's about alignment. If team accountability is critical to how you demonstrate leadership prowess, then it should be reflected in how you communicate, show up, and respond to challenges. Some leaders even bring in external partners to help galvanize a new or renewed culture of shared responsibility across the organization.

A powerful example of this is Dean Eggers, whose belief in a culture of accountability is evident in how he leads his team and the School of Professional Studies. In return, the school community and leadership team hold him accountable—not in a punitive way, but through a shared commitment to excellence. Accountability becomes mutual and meaningful when the impact of success is felt collectively, as it is by the students, faculty, and staff at his school.

If your organization already has a strong culture of accountability, reinforce it by creating consistent, structured ways for your team to engage in honest conversations. Share your own challenges. Invite feedback. Listen without judgment. And model the truth that accountability flows in both directions.

Be intentional about creating psychological safety. Ensure that your conversations are confidential, trusted, and affirming— so every team member feels safe, valued, and supported. Let them take the lead in defining how they want to be held accountable. Accountability works best when it's co-created, not imposed.

Team accountability is often discussed in LinkedIn's Contributors community, where leaders regularly exchange insights on how to cultivate it effectively. Two themes always rise to the top: psychological safety and trust.

This habit is not only about building culture but also about cultivating trust, transparency, and a team that feels seen, heard, and respected. When done well, everyone rises together.

The myth of leadership perfection is a relic of the past. Today's most effective leaders are not afraid to show emotion. They lead with empathy, clarity, humility, and a spirit of service. When you rise, your team rises with you. This sense of communal accountability becomes a driving force behind innovation, loyalty, and high-performing teams that understand the power of mutual investment.

As author and leadership coach Jack Ricchiuto writes in *The Mindful Leader* (2024), "People learn to feel, perform, and interact differently when supported by mindful leaders"—the opposite of what happens under mindless ones.

Habits like this are foundational to living an earned life: one rooted in perspective, learning, and intentional leadership. It's the kind of life—and leadership—that inspires others, drives meaningful results, and turns every mistake into an opportunity for growth.

Building a culture of mutual accountability starts with leadership modeling, fosters psychological safety and trust, and empowers teams to grow, collaborate, and rise together.

Habit 8: Partner with a Professional Coach for Accountability

Partnering with a professional coach requires both a time investment and a psychological commitment. It becomes a powerful habit only when you're truly ready to do the work: to reflect deeply, take consistent action, and embrace growth with intention.

Begin by reviewing your leadership prowess self-assessment results. What patterns or gaps stand out? Which areas of your leadership need attention, development, or refinement? These insights can help you clarify the kind of coach you need and how to enter the partnership with focus and purpose.

A professional coach isn't there to give you all the answers— they're there to walk beside you, ask the right questions, help reveal blind spots, and hold you accountable for the goals you set. When the partnership is intentional and aligned, it can accelerate your growth, sharpen your leadership presence, and expand your self-awareness.

Coaching is a habit-forming leadership practice because it builds a rhythm of reflection, accountability, and supported growth. A coach provides a space of trust where you are both challenged and encouraged. This is a hallmark of leadership maturity and a powerful act of vulnerability. Now is the time to make coaching a habit that extends your leadership and brings your leadership prowess into action.

■ ■ ■

In Part 3 of this book, we'll explore coaching prowess, a framework designed to help leaders understand what it means to be coachable, how to nurture others effectively, how to humanize the coaching experience, and how to apply the leadership in action pyramid for lasting impact.

PART 3

Embracing Coaching Prowess

7

What Is Coaching Prowess?

Coaching Prowess: The Power to Inspire

Have you ever met someone who, after just a few minutes of conversation, leaves you feeling deeply inspired? Sometimes, even years later, encountering them again can reignite that same feeling.

If you ask Marshall's coaching clients and MG100 community, they would all say the same about him. Jack Canfield, author and leadership expert, is also known for having this kind of impact.

But have you ever wondered why certain individuals are so profoundly inspirational? What leadership qualities or personal traits enable them to influence others so deeply and meaningfully?

That lasting, uplifting influence is what we call *coaching prowess*: the ability to inspire, empower, and motivate others to grow beyond what they believed possible.

At its core is *nurturing*: a presence that not only uplifts but also strengthens and sustains. Nurturing is the third pillar of the WIN mindset model, and it lies at the heart of *coaching prowess*—the focus of this final section of this book.

141

In today's ever-evolving work environments, leaders must learn to balance influence, results, and team support with a nurturing presence, one that enables others to grow, thrive, and lead with confidence, even in the leader's absence.

We define *coaching prowess* as the ability—and the desire—to nurture, support, and develop others to reach their fullest potential, especially during times of uncertainty and fluctuations.

To nurture is to care. It's the human skill at the core of impactful, resilient leadership. It means providing the space, encouragement, and accountability necessary for personal and collective success. In an era of rising competition, uncertainty, and complexity, nurturing leadership isn't optional—it's essential.

To help leaders understand the full scope of coaching prowess and its deep connection to nurturing, we introduce the leadership in action pyramid (see Figure 7.1), a framework designed to guide reflection, growth, and practice. The pyramid is structured on three tiers:

- Care for self
- Align with purpose
- Nurture others

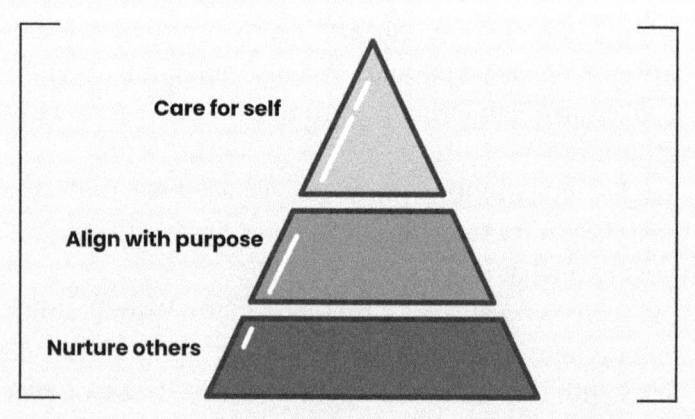

FIGURE 7.1 The leadership in action pyramid.

Together, these elements form the foundation for leading with authenticity, compassion, and lasting impact. If you've ever met a leader who deeply inspires you, it's likely because they've done the inner work—nurturing themselves, aligning with their purpose, and committing to the growth of others.

You're here because you're on a similar path. The fact that you've picked up this book and arrived at this chapter is proof: you're ready to lead with intention and align your leadership prowess with coaching prowess.

At first glance, the leadership in action pyramid might suggest that great leaders naturally master all three tiers at once: care for self, align with purpose, and nurture others. And while that may be the aspiration, the truth is few leaders begin that way. Most can't lead others effectively until they've first learned how to care for themselves.

Care for Self

The foundation of coaching prowess—and the foundation of impactful leadership—starts with the first tier: care for self. To care for oneself is to acknowledge and tend to all parts of who we are, especially the uneven parts we often overlook, suppress, or rush past.

In our work with leaders just beginning this journey, we often sense a quiet, unspoken longing for something deeper. Even when they can't articulate it, the feeling is there—from the very first conversation. It reveals itself as a hunger for clarity, meaning, and inner alignment.

That's why the first tier of the pyramid—*care for self*—is so essential. It's where the real work begins. It's where leaders learn to pause, listen inwardly, and take the first step toward wholeness.

To lead is to work, and to lead impactful teams requires ongoing reflection and personal check-ins. Leaders must learn to nurture the uneven, often overlooked parts of themselves if they hope to inspire meaningful action and connection in others.

In *Flying Without a Net* (Harvard Business Review Press, 2011), author Thomas J. DeLong explores how shifting workplace demands can quietly erode a leader's sense of self. He calls this *organizational failure*: when companies aim to provide a sense of purpose and identity but fall short due to a disconnect between their intentions and the lived experience of their people.

Take Reka, a high-performing chief strategist hired to lead global expansion at a pharmaceutical company. She thrived in the role until market pressures prompted leadership to shift her responsibilities toward sales strategy, an area well outside her expertise or passion.

As her role changed, so did her connection to the work. She no longer felt anchored in purpose. Over time, the misalignment wore her down. Her performance declined, her health suffered, and the once-clear leader her team relied on began to fade.

Reka lost herself and lost her ability to care for herself. Under the pressure to maintain the same momentum and reputation she had once earned, she struggled silently, attempting to adjust to the new demands so as not to let her leaders down.

She believed she was hiding it well. But the truth is, everyone noticed, because leadership is visible. As imperfect as leaders may be, their missteps are public, and their good intentions are on display, too.

Reka's story is not uncommon. Many leaders face shifting roles and rising demands—often without anyone asking how they're doing or checking in on the support they need. They move from task to task, role to role, without pausing to reflect. Over time, that disconnect deepens.

It's natural for leaders to stumble early in their journey. But you can't stay in that space for too long. Once you feel the weight of work and life bearing down, ask yourself the most important question, "How am I taking care of myself? Am I still in control, or have I lost control over my own care?"

Coaching prowess begins with self-leadership. It's the ability to coach yourself through the daily grind, the highs, the lows, and everything in between. When that becomes difficult, it's a signal to turn to your leadership accountability scale, your trusted support system and internal compass.

Reka's story is not unique. Many leaders quietly wrestle with shifting responsibilities and unclear expectations. What we often fail to recognize is this: work consumes the majority of our time—arguably most of our lives. That's why nurturing yourself is not a luxury; it's a necessity.

The emotional and physical toll of leadership is real. Without a commitment to self-care, you won't have the capacity to care for anything—or anyone—else. Don't make the mistake of believing you can live in survival mode forever. Leaders are not meant to just survive; they're meant to thrive. And when the role becomes unclear, thriving means knowing how to pause, reassess, and pivot.

Leadership begins with how you manage yourself. If you want to inspire others—if you want your influence to be real and lasting—you must commit to taking care of yourself especially when you feel the tension piling up. The decision to pause and care for yourself is not weakness; it's one of the most powerful acts of leadership.

Leaders are givers by design. And when you're unable to give, the consequences are deeper and more damaging than most realize. That's why the first and most important gift you can offer—your team, your mission, and yourself—is your own well-being and knowing when to prioritize care for self.

Let's consider the experience of a leader named Michael. He always loved working with people but never expected to step into leadership so quickly. Fresh out of his MBA program, he joined a nonprofit, eager to learn on the job. When the organization recognized his strong leadership potential and decisive empathy, they quickly promoted him to director of external affairs.

But Michael struggled. He didn't feel ready for the role and was afraid to speak up about his challenges. His confidence waned, and those around him noticed the shift—from a poised, assured professional to someone uncertain in his decisions and actions.

Leaders who regularly check in with themselves lead more sustainably. They don't just chase goals, they stay anchored in meaning. They model resilience not by pushing through at all costs, but by knowing when to pause, reflect, and replenish.

You might think Michael's struggle is no surprise—after all, he's early in his career. But similar challenges arise for seasoned leaders too, even newly appointed CEOs. The truth is, leadership struggles are not always about experience; they're often about capacity and care.

The lesson is this: never abandon the need to care for yourself—even when others begin to recognize and reward your potential. Being chosen or promoted isn't always about proven outcomes; often, it's your consistent actions, decisive mindset, and the character traits that signal promise. But sustaining that promise requires inner alignment.

Coaching prowess begins by tending to the uneven parts within, especially when the stakes are high and expectations even higher. It begins by learning to listen inwardly before leading outwardly. Without this foundation, the desire to nurture others risks becoming performative or obligatory. With it, you lead with clarity, depth, and a grounded presence others naturally trust.

That's why the first tier of coaching prowess is *care for self*. It's not self-indulgence—it's self-honesty. It's the discipline of creating space to acknowledge the uneven, overlooked, or unspoken parts of yourself. The parts you've ignored in pursuit of performance. The parts still aching for clarity, healing, or recognition.

Caring for self includes physical well-being, yes, but it also demands emotional awareness, purpose alignment, and mental stillness. It invites you to pause and ask these questions:

- Who am I right now?
- What is happening to me at this moment?
- What anxieties am I confronting?
- What kind of support do I need?

Again, leaders who regularly check in with themselves lead more sustainably. They don't just set goals, they root their actions in meaning. They model resilience not by powering through but by knowing when and how to replenish.

Those who embrace this habit create the conditions to move into the second tier of the Leadership in action pyramid: align with purpose.

Align with Purpose

- Are you aligned with your purpose?
- Does the work you do today reflect the values and vision you hold most deeply?
- And does that alignment matter to you?

These are not rhetorical questions; they are essential checkpoints. And while the answers may not come easily or quickly, they deserve thoughtful reflection. Take your time. Be honest. Return to them if you must, but come with reflective responses.

In the practice of coaching prowess, aligning with purpose is not optional, it is foundational. It's the bridge between caring for self and being able to effectively nurture others. Without this alignment, even the most well-intentioned leaders risk operating from a place of disconnection or burnout.

Purpose is your internal compass—it guides your decisions, regulates your emotions, and fuels your ambition and aspirations. It helps you lead with conviction, empathy, and a grounded presence. Leaders with coaching prowess revisit and refine their purpose often—especially in seasons of transition, uncertainty, or growth. When you're anchored in purpose, your leadership becomes both visible and uplifting to those near and far.

A powerful example of purpose alignment is Charlamagne tha God (Lenard McKelvey), cohost of *The Breakfast Club* on iHeart-Radio, which reaches over six million listeners each month.

When his life began to drift off course, he made the intentional decision to realign with something deep and that aligned with his passion. The journey wasn't easy, but his clarity of intention and commitment to growth helped him rise to become one of the most influential voices in media.

Known for his provocative style, Charlamagne remains unapologetically authentic. He often credits his discipline and entrepreneurial mindset to lessons learned from his father. He also speaks openly about how therapy has helped him care for himself and adjust his behavior in real time.

His story is a powerful reminder that aligning with purpose isn't about perfection—it's about self-awareness, authenticity, and the willingness to grow and nurture the parts of ourselves that others don't always see.

Most leaders strive for purpose alignment, yet it's easy to lose focus—whether due to a life event, failure, or personal disappointment. The truth is, nothing in life is perfect. That's why managing our internal expectations for perfectionism is so important.

Many leaders are, in fact, close to their purpose—but because they struggle to trust themselves or fail to nurture their inner world, they overlook the treasures already within reach.

Aligning with purpose begins with curiosity. It starts by looking around and asking, "Am I missing something? Do I desire something more?" Then, dare to imagine what *more* could look like—realistically and intentionally. Life is not abstract; it is lived in real time. And everything you do holds weight and meaning. Purpose isn't just an ideal—it's a lived, daily practice.

Let's look at an example of an executive aligning with her purpose. Christine had finally landed her dream role—chief marketing officer at one of the top global consumer brands. For her, it was the ultimate expression of purpose fulfilled. She had worked long hours, delivered consistently, and now it had all paid off.

She loved the culture, admired her leadership team, and had earned the coveted corner office—complete with its own private bathroom and a sweeping 16th-floor view of New York City. Christine was thriving, aligned with her purpose, and watching her dreams come to life.

Then, she was invited to join the board of a nonprofit dedicated to providing job training for low-income young professionals with limited access to role models. Eventually, Christine became chair of the board and led the charge to raise the organization's first $1 million in funding.

Her success with the nonprofit filled her with pride—but something else began to stir. Back at work, she found her thoughts drifting. She wondered what more she could do for the nonprofit. Her passion for the cause grew.

One day, during a leadership team meeting, Christine shared her involvement with the nonprofit. Her colleagues were impressed by her commitment and impact. But in articulating her role and aspirations for the organization, something shifted inside her.

The energy she once reserved for her corporate career now gravitated toward the mission of the nonprofit. Slowly, her momentum at work began to wane. She felt less anchored in what had once been her dream. Her sense of purpose had evolved—and so had she.

Christine wasn't entirely sure what was shifting within her, but she felt a quiet misalignment stirring deep inside. Seeking understanding, she turned to a licensed coach. Through their conversations, she came to realize that her purpose had changed—her commitment to the nonprofit board had quietly reshaped her dreams and her sense of fulfillment. When asked what she wanted to do next, her answer came gently but firmly: she wanted to dedicate herself to the charity full-time.

Sometimes, when a leader loses alignment with their purpose, it's not the workplace's fault. No one is to blame for changing desires. Purpose evolves—and that evolution is a natural part of growth. Christine had invested 10 years in her company and reached what many would consider the pinnacle of her career. Yet within that achievement, she discovered a deeper truth: purpose is fluid, and it's okay for it to find new ground.

Leadership, like life, is a journey of continual realignment. It's okay to forge new paths—for your career, your calling, and your well-being. Just be sure to involve your leadership accountability partners—those you trust to offer honest feedback and perspective as you navigate change. Take your time in deciding what feels true for you. Sometimes, realignment with purpose requires deep reflection and the right partners to walk that process with you.

Christine eventually resigned from her dream job and accepted a position with the nonprofit organization. In this new role, she thrived—personally and professionally—and was deeply fulfilled by the impact of her work. She was not only content with her choice but also genuinely thrilled by it.

The lesson here is simple yet profound: listen to yourself. Pay attention to your reactions, your energy, and the quiet shifts happening within. The goal of aligning with purpose is to help you take ownership of your life's direction—what you're experiencing internally and what's evolving in real time.

But alignment isn't about impulsiveness; it's about being intentional and realistic with your choices. This is what it means to live your truth—in real life, not just in theory. It's also what happens when you stop ignoring the uneven parts of yourself.

To be an inspirational leader is to know and love who you are and to honor who you are becoming as life continues to evolve.

So we ask you these questions:

- Do you sense a shift within you?
- What is prompting this change?
- Are you aligned with your purpose?
- Are you truly living your truth right now?

Nurture Others

Leadership is a gift that extends outward. Caring for oneself and aligning with purpose are essential foundations, but the true test of coaching prowess lies in the third tier: the ability to nurture others. Inspirational leaders don't just drive results—they invest in the people around them. They notice potential, make space for growth, and commit to lifting others as they lead.

If you've ever had the privilege of working with a leader who truly nurtures others, consider yourself fortunate. The reality is, many leaders are still operating from the first or second tier: focused on caring for themselves or working to align with their own purpose. In that space, they may not yet have the capacity to offer their team the kind of leadership nurture that empowers everyone to rise together.

You might be wondering, "Why do organizations hire such individuals?" The truth is, many organizations are simply unaware of the leadership in action pyramid as a barometer for truly inspirational leadership. Often, these leaders are doing the best they can with what they have. But when tier one and tier two are incomplete or neglected, they create an invisible barrier to nurturing others.

Over time, teams may come to accept the reality of imperfect leadership because expecting perfection is unrealistic. And while perfection isn't the goal, the expectation still stands: all leaders should learn to nurture their teams. Not flawlessly, but intentionally. Not all at once, but with care and commitment.

We want to share three leadership stories featuring distinctly different leaders: Richard, Taylor, and Maya. Richard was recently promoted to the C-suite and approached the role with excitement and anticipation.

Taylor and Maya, however, were seasoned C-suite executives shaped by years of experience. While Taylor and Maya worked within the same company, Richard came from a different organization and held a different functional role. Each of their stories offers a unique lens on what it means to lead, adapt, and nurture, especially during moments of transition and self-leadership.

Richard was known throughout the organization for building strong, innovative teams that consistently delivered great results. However, when he was promoted to the C-suite, he was assigned a completely new team, one he hadn't been involved in hiring.

As a result, he didn't feel as connected to them. Richard struggled to motivate the team and tried to nurture them using the same tactics that had worked so well with his previous group. As Marshall famously expressed in his first book, *What Got You Here Won't Get You There: How Successful People Become Even More Successful* (Grand Central Publishing, 2007), "What got you here won't get you there," and Richard's story illustrates this perfectly.

Richard later realized he needed to revisit his leadership in action pyramid to be effective in his new role and with his new team. He began by returning to the basics: caring for himself, then aligning his purpose with that of his team.

This foundation enabled him to genuinely nurture his team. He scheduled one-on-one sessions with each team member to check on their well-being, understand their goals, uncover their challenges, and learn about the shortcomings of their previous leader.

In caring for himself, Richard evolved into an executive coach, recognizing that succeeding in his new role required authentic learning and growth. His coach used Marshall's stakeholder-centered coaching model, designed to help leaders achieve lasting change, and conducted 360-degree interviews with each member of Richard's team.

The feedback was initially tough to hear—brutal, even—but Richard saw it as a vital starting point to realign with his team and unify their shared sense of purpose. His team was worth the investment. This honest reflection, combined with his commitment to understanding both his new team and how his leadership was evolving paved the way for deeper connection, renewed trust, and more aligned leadership.

The lesson here is crucial for all leaders: while reaching all three tiers is a goal, life changes and new roles require us to reassess and adapt. Remember, what got you here won't get you there—at least not without the willingness to learn, intentional leadership, and a genuine desire to nurture others.

Taylor had been with the company for 17 years and, as a seasoned C-suite executive, he was deeply aligned with its mission and values. But when senior leadership informed him of a relocation to another country, everything shifted. On arrival, Taylor quickly realized that his influence didn't carry the same weight in this new territory. The team dynamics were different, and cultural nuances affected communication and collaboration.

As project targets slipped and misalignment grew, Taylor's initial instinct was to replace the entire team. Known for nurturing his previous teams, he now found himself prioritizing performance over people. He began hiring based on his personal preferences, seeking talent that matched his previous team's style and pace. The pressure mounted, and the existing team watched in fear as colleagues were replaced, sometimes for minor mistakes or dips in performance.

By the end of the second quarter, nearly everyone on Taylor's original team—except for his administrative support—had been replaced. You might be wondering whether it was necessary for Taylor to rebuild the entire team due to early misalignment. Was it fair to dismiss team members over performance struggles that may have been rooted in adaptation, lack of mentorship, or coaching prowess? Could there have been a better way to lead through the transition—one grounded in understanding, development, nurture, and trust?

Leaders should have the freedom to make decisions as they see fit in a given situation. However, the expectation is that they try to use frameworks—like the *leadership in action pyramid*—to assess their positionality, leadership approach, and team-nurturing strategy, especially when stepping into a new environment with unfamiliar dynamics.

Taylor's actions also stood in contrast to Marshall Goldsmith's principle: what got you here won't get you there. In this case, if Taylor had used the leadership in action pyramid to reflect on what was shifting internally—his expectations, emotions, and pressure—and begin with the foundational tier, care for self. This could have involved seeking support from a coach, trusted colleague, or accountability partner.

What Taylor didn't recognize was that his new team was also adjusting to his leadership style, cultural differences, and the weight of transition. There was a disconnect not just in performance but also in communication and trust. No one asked how they were doing. No one created space for open dialogue. And without that, the opportunity to build cohesion through coaching prowess was missed.

What Taylor didn't know was that another seasoned C-suite executive from his company, Maya, had also been relocated to lead a team in an international division. Like Taylor, Maya stepped into unfamiliar territory and was met with hesitation and distance from her new team. But instead of assuming the issue was rooted in poor performance, Maya took a different approach—she paused and turned inward.

She began with the first tier of the leadership in action pyramid: care for self. She reflected on how the transition was affecting her personally: What assumptions was she bringing into this new role? What fears or frustrations was she carrying? She spoke with a coach, journaled daily, and focused on staying grounded in her values.

Next, she focused on aligning with purpose. She revisited why she took this new assignment and clarified what kind of leader she wanted to be in this new chapter. Her purpose wasn't just to "perform"—it was to build trust, create belonging, and leave a legacy of empowered leadership.

Finally, Maya stepped into the third tier: nurturing others. She scheduled one-on-one meetings with each team member, not to evaluate performance but to listen, understand, and begin building meaningful connections.

She asked these questions:

- What do you need to do your best work here?
- What excites or worries you about the direction we're headed?
- What do you want me to understand about this team's culture or history?

Rather than replacing her team, she chose to reinvest in them. And over time, trust grew. Performance improved. And her team began to see her not as a distant executive but as a partner in their shared success.

The three stories share common threads: they each explore what great leaders face in the workplace. But what sets them apart is how each leader responds to change and the pursuit of something deeper: a more fulfilled, authentic version of themselves.

Richard and Maya's sense of happiness stems from their genuine desire to win *with* their teams, not just *through* them. Taylor, however, was driven by a desire to win at all costs. Rather than adapting to the new environment, he clung to his old habits and leadership style, approaching the challenge as though it required a full reset—a more entrepreneurial, start-over mentality.

Coaching Prowess Is Being a Courageous Leader

Courageous leadership starts by looking within. It is not about being fearless but about choosing growth over comfort, empathy over ego, and authenticity over performance.

This isn't to say that every leader must force a fit with every team, but it is to say this: when you're reassigned, promoted, or placed in a new environment, the first step isn't outward—it's inward. Begin with reflection before initiating change. Tap into your leadership accountability networks or trusted partners.

The true foundation of leadership begins with coaching prowess, and at the heart of that prowess is the ability to nurture. Nurturing leaders drive action, foster motivation, and build genuine partnerships from within. They also create cultures grounded in accountability, leadership in action, and the visible courage of vulnerability.

This is your opportunity to invite your new team to help you win—together. To co-create a bond strong enough to weather any storm.

For many leaders, the behaviors they display on the job are rooted in lessons once taught—habits inherited from past mentors, experiences, or organizational cultures. While some of these patterns may have been effective at one time, not all are meant to be carried forward.

When your leadership starts to echo outdated approaches that yield limited or even negative outcomes, take it as a signal. The goal isn't to keep pushing through unchanged—it's to pause, reflect, and pursue something deeper and more aligned with who you are becoming.

This is where Marshall's lesson—what got you here won't get you there—rings true: the actions that brought you success in the past may no longer be enough to get you where you want to go today. The leadership in action pyramid offers a framework to help you assess where you are today and where you want to go:

- Are you caring for self?
- Are you aligning with purpose?
- Are you nurturing others?

We could argue that Taylor's actions served only himself. Operating solely at tier one is never enough to become an effective, transformative, or inspiring leader.

So ask yourself these questions:

- Who do I want to be in this new space?
- What leadership attributes do I want to be recognized for?
- Does it matter how my team or organization experiences my decisions—and how those decisions affect the people I was meant to uplift, nurture, and lead?

Coaching Prowess Shapes Our Leadership Legacy

Leadership legacy begins now, not just in the later stages of life. It's about shaping our attitudes, habits, leadership practices, and responses in every moment.

Great leadership goes beyond driving performance; it's about nurturing potential, both within ourselves and in those we lead. As seen in the journeys of Richard, Taylor, and Maya, every leader faces moments that challenge their adaptability, clarity, and compassion. What sets truly inspirational leaders apart is not perfection, but their commitment to reflect inwardly before leading outwardly.

Coaching prowess is the thread that weaves it all together. It's the quiet discipline of self-reflection. The courageous choice to lead with care, even when it's difficult. And the boldness to model growth, vulnerability, and trust.

So, ask yourself these questions:

- Who am I becoming as a leader?
- How am I caring for my team—and for myself?
- What kind of culture am I nurturing around me?

At the end of the day, nurturing isn't a leadership add-on—it *is* the work. And when you nurture well, you don't just lead teams, you shape futures. That's how leadership legacy is formed: not only through strategy and success but also through care, presence, and intentional growth. It becomes the identity you carry and the impact you leave behind—something recognizable, meaningful, and magnetic. It's a kind of leadership others feel in your presence and often aspire to model in their own journey.

Leadership is visible, impactful, and unforgettable. People experience it—directly or indirectly—through every interaction. That's why it's wise to use reflective tools like the leadership in action pyramid to adjust your lens, hold yourself accountable, and recognize when you're slipping into self-preservation instead of service.

A Final Lesson from an Unexpected Place

A surprising but powerful example of leadership comes from an episode of *Teenage Mutant Ninja Turtles*. After Splinter appointed Leonardo as the team's leader, the turtles were sent on a high-stakes mission to rescue someone held captive by Shredder. Leonardo, determined to prove himself, went off alone—and failed. He was paralyzed in battle and had to be rescued by his brothers.

After reviving him, Raphael shouting at Leonardo, as he tries to express his disapproval of leaders who prefers to work independent of their teams, stating that instead the role of the leader is to lead a team, not just lead themselves. In response, Leonard immediately apologized, acknowledging his leadership mistake.

That moment captures the essence of real leadership. It's not about proving yourself in isolation; it's about guiding, empowering, and showing up with and for your team. *Teenage Mutant Ninja Turtles*, though animated, has become a globally recognized story not just for its action, but for its emphasis on teamwork, individual growth, and shared purpose.

Leadership legacy isn't built on solo victories. It's built on trust, connection, and the willingness to admit when you need others. When you lead with courage, care, and coaching prowess, your team will rise with you—and stand by you when you fall.

If you're aiming to create a legacy of prowess, intentional leadership, and care, then every moment is a powerful opportunity to practice that commitment. Start now. Lead well. Lead together.

8

Why Should Leaders Embrace Coaching?

What the Greatest Athletes Teach Us About Coaching

The world's greatest athletes—across every era, every field, and every country—share one essential trait: they all had great coaches. Think of legends like Babe Ruth, Michael Jordan, Kobe Bryant, LeBron James, Venus and Serena Williams, Jackie Robinson, Derek Jeter, Nadia Comaneci, Alex Rodriguez, Lionel Messi, Pelé, Cristiano Ronaldo, Diego Maradona, David Beckham, Abby Wambach, Alex Morgan, Sun Wen, Mia Hamm, Megan Rapinoe, Marta—and the list goes on.

Regardless of their sport or individual brilliance, these athletes didn't get to the top alone. They trained with discipline, they studied the game, they pushed through failure, and they all had one or more coaches guiding their path.

We'll save the conversation about teams and affiliations for later, because while team chemistry matters, this section focuses on what makes these athletes dynamic, precise, and consistently high-performing. It's their relationship with coaching. In interviews, memoirs, and moments of reflection, many of them credit their longevity, growth, and clutch performances to the guidance and accountability of exceptional coaches.

There are levels to great coaching—and as leaders, we're not just looking to admire these relationships. We're asking a deeper question: how can you become that kind of coach for yourself, for your team, and for your organization?

Being an exceptional coach isn't just about giving feedback or leading meetings. It's about unlocking performance, nurturing potential, and holding space for growth under pressure. It's also about doing the hard work and setting the pace.

With everything in life, it's through practice and reflection that we uncover our potential—and that includes discovering the great coach within you. Coaching, at its core, is about creating the moments and conditions for both growth and greatness, in yourself and in others.

Think of it like parenting: when a child succeeds, the parents are praised. But when the child struggles, people often question the parents. The same logic applies to coaching. When athletes perform at their peak, coaches and teams are celebrated. But when things go wrong, the conversation shifts—criticism often falls on the coach before anyone else.

Of course, with the rise of social media, these dynamics have evolved. Now, the scrutiny is immediate and everywhere— online debates, TV commentary, and radio discussions dissect every win and loss, every strategy and misstep. Performance is public, and so is the judgment.

But here's the point: everyone notices when things work—or don't. And in sports, much of the credit (or blame) goes to the coach. That's not to diminish the raw talent, dedication, or natural ability of the athletes themselves. Some are born with extraordinary gifts, others develop theirs through discipline, repetition, and sustained investment over time.

Still, behind every consistent, high-performing athlete is a coach: someone who helps shape the athlete's path, mindset, discoveries, and outcome.

Now, some of you might argue that coaches don't always get to choose their teams. Often, they inherit a group of players they didn't select themselves—and that's true. But the same principle applies: the world still holds the coach accountable for the team's transformation and success. Today, anyone can weigh in—fans, analysts, commentators—publicly evaluating a coach's ability to turn potential into performance.

What Team Movies Teach Us About Coaching

We've seen this narrative reflected countless times on screen. Some of the most powerful sports films capture what it takes for a determined coach to take a struggling or underestimated team and transform them into champions. These movies don't just entertain; they reveal deep truths about coaching, leadership, and belief. Some standout examples include *Remember the Titans*, *Coach Carter*, *The Mighty Ducks*, *Hoosiers*, and others.

Each of these stories shows us that coaching isn't about perfection, trophies, or winning. It often begins with a lack of wins—a hunger for growth—and from that hunger, something powerful begins to take shape. Trust builds. Momentum follows. The team starts to believe. And that's when the magic happens.

Coaching is about persistence, empathy, vision, and care. These same qualities are at the heart of exceptional leadership— whether on the field, in the boardroom, or out in the world. They've been central to the themes we've explored throughout this book, and they're also traits we hope to distill in you.

As you lead your team, we invite you to think, act, and become a coach—one who sees their team as capable of greatness. A coach who knows how to nurture that greatness into action.

For many of us, watching sports is thrilling not just because of the competition, but because of the layers beneath it: someone will win—yes—but how they win, who steps up, how the team moves together, and the silent choreography between coach and player is what truly captivates.

We watch the high fives, the intensity, the subtle nods of encouragement. We notice when a coach raises their arms in triumph or lowers their head in quiet reflection. We feel the tension when a player gets hurt and the unspoken connection between coach and team. Even without knowing the score, we can often predict the outcome—because the body language and energy of the coach says everything.

What We Discovered About Coaching in the Workplace

In many workplaces, coaching is often reserved for high-potential employees. Why? Because, frankly, most leaders are overwhelmed: burned out, overworked, and stretched too thin to offer consistent coaching to every member of their team. Some leaders assume that hiring top talent means the need for coaching disappears, that high performers will simply continue to produce at high levels. But that's a dangerous myth. Every great sports coach knows that even the most elite athlete must be nurtured, challenged, and supported, or their talent will eventually diminish.

Some leaders begin as strong coaches but get distracted or discouraged when the return on investment isn't immediately visible. They pause their coaching efforts to focus on what they deem "more pressing matters." Others give up on the team members they've mentally labeled as weak links, shifting their energy elsewhere. In some cases, leaders transfer these lower-performing individuals to other departments or lay them off, and reward only the top performers with opportunities for growth.

But here's what often gets missed: leadership is visible.

Everyone sees what you're doing—even when they don't say anything. Your team, your peers, your organization—they're all observing. And when you're not in the room, they're having conversations about your leadership, whether in admiration or disappointment. Just like spectators at a sports game, they're assessing how you lead, where your attention goes, and what kind of leader you truly are.

It's no different from the classroom. When a professor is excellent, students talk—and word spreads quickly about how inspiring that professor is. But when the experience is poor, students talk about that too, in detail. The same applies to leadership in any space: your actions are being watched, interpreted, and talked about—often quietly, but consistently.

In some cases, even when leaders make the effort to coach, team members may not respond favorably. The discomfort of receiving direct, constructive feedback can cause some individuals to disengage. Over time, both the leader and the team member may begin meeting less frequently, and the opportunity for growth gradually fades.

The good news? Most leaders understand that coaching isn't optional—it's essential. They recognize that how they show up as a coach directly shapes how their leadership is perceived, experienced, and remembered.

But here's something worth exploring; whether they struggle or excel, most leaders have one thing in common: a strong desire to create an environment where their teams can grow, thrive, and perform at their highest potential. The leaders who coach prioritize it. Those who struggle often do so because of time constraints, competing demands, or a lack of clarity on how to coach effectively.

What's often left unspoken is this: many leaders never received great coaching themselves. So how can we expect them to model something they were never taught or exposed to?

To that, we say: let's change that narrative. Let's equip you with the tools to become the best coach for your team. And that journey starts where all great coaching begins—with learning how to coach yourself.

Learning to Coach Yourself

Sometimes, the best place to start is within.

In *The Light We Carry* (Crown Publishing, 2022), Michelle Obama shares a story about her friend's husband, Ron, who spoke to himself in the mirror every morning. He had done it for years, unaware that his wife could hear him as she quietly lay in bed. What stood out wasn't just the act itself—but the intention behind it. Michelle would later describe this practice as "starting kind."

Each morning, many of us pass by a mirror without realizing the power it holds—not just to reflect our image but also to reflect our inner dialogue. For Michelle, Ron's habit became a new way to begin her mornings: by turning the light inward and choosing to see beyond self-criticism or flaw-finding. She embraced a more compassionate, grounding way to face the day.

There's something profoundly powerful about how we manage ourselves when no one is watching. These quiet rituals—how we motivate, redirect, affirm, or reflect—are often the clearest expressions of self-leadership. They reveal how we build resilience, how we grant ourselves grace, and how we prepare for what lies ahead.

Patrick Mouratoglou, the renowned mental coach known for guiding players to multiple Grand Slam titles—including Serena Williams and Coco Gauff—shared in his book *Champion Mindset* (Workman Publishing, 2025) that none of his successes with athletes would have been possible if he hadn't first won the internal battle for his own happiness, purpose, and sense of meaning.

Learning to coach yourself begins with paying attention to how you speak to yourself. Be mindful; self-coaching is not about arrogance or dismissiveness. It's not about striving for perfection, either. It's about becoming your own mirror, one that reflects not only what is, but what's possible. It's about asking the hard questions, practicing emotional discipline, and holding yourself accountable to the future you're working to create.

If speaking kindly to yourself feels difficult, that's okay. You may benefit from seeking support from a licensed therapist or mental health professional. Recognizing when you need additional tools is not a weakness; it's a powerful form of self-management. It's a sign that you are showing up for yourself, which is essential if you hope to meaningfully show up for others.

What sets great coaches apart is often their lived experience: the challenges they've overcome and the intentional ways they've coached themselves along the way. In fact, many of the world's most celebrated athletic coaches were once athletes themselves. Their journey inward became the foundation for how they inspire, challenge, and lead others.

Start with Daily Drills

Just like athletes, great leaders benefit from daily drills. The idea isn't just about physical movement; it's about intentional, repeated actions that build strength, discipline, and clarity.

For athletes, drills are a mix of solo and team-based exercises: running laps, practicing formations, refining techniques. These activities aren't glamorous, but they're essential to performance. The same principle applies to leadership. What are your daily drills: the intentional habits that ground you, sharpen your mindset, and strengthen your capacity to lead?

Whether it's morning reflection, journaling, mindful breathing, time blocking, reading affirmations, music, or even reviewing goals for the day—daily drills create space for calm and focus in the midst of pressure. For leaders who spend their days managing people, time, deadlines, and deliverables, these micro-practices offer essential moments to reset and realign.

In his book, *Flying Without a Net* (Harvard Business Review Press, 2011), Harvard Business School Professor Thomas DeLong shares how many high-performing leaders struggle silently with anxiety, often suppressing it in workplaces where vulnerability is misunderstood or judged. Much of this anxiety stems from internal questions:

- Am I producing enough?
- Does my boss still value me?
- Does my team respect me?
- Am I still considered one of the top leaders here?

Without daily grounding practices, these worries can spiral and deplete your energy. But with a consistent drill—your own version of a mental warm-up—you can begin the day with clarity and confidence. You can also create a plan to address some of the things that are on your mind or address the matters that consume your mental strength.

See your drills as rehearsal. We're not suggesting that leadership is performative, but we *are* suggesting that you treat your leadership and coaching practice as a way to strengthen and refine your performance as a leader.

Rehearsal is essential to every great performance. History is full of examples showing how the world's best performers—from athletes to artists—prioritize time to rehearse. We've all heard famous affirmations like: "The champ is here," or "You got this." These mantras are more than words; they are drills for the mind.

So, choose a phrase or ritual that works for you. One that grounds you. Activates you. Motivates you to lead from your highest self.

Something we've observed, having spoken on stages around the world, is that even seasoned speakers have drills. A moment. A mantra. A movement. It's how we awaken the inner part of ourselves that's ready to be fully present and fully accountable.

Find your drill—make it personal, private, and sacred. Use it when you're reaching for your next level or simply when you need a quiet reminder to start kind.

Becoming the Coach Your Team Needs

As leaders, we don't always say it out loud, but we want our teams to need us. We crave their trust, affection, and attention just as much as they seek ours. We want to be the kind of leader they'll remember—as someone who believed in them, challenged them, nurtured them, and brought out their best.

Ultimately, we want to strive to be their greatest coach.

But somewhere along the way, the stamina it takes to show up consistently—with care, clarity, intention, and conviction—can begin to wear thin. The demands build. Our energy dips. The fire dims. And we find ourselves quietly wondering: how do I keep fueling my team when I feel like I'm running on empty?

Our advice: return to your learning prowess. Recognize when it's time to invest in the inner work—learning, relearning, and upskilling—to grow into the leader your team needs next.

Recenter your energy by asking yourself these questions: Is this a moment to recharge so I can become what is required of me next? Or is this a moment to lead even when my energy doesn't match the momentum I once had?

Our good friend and executive coach Connie Dieken joined more than 120 senior leaders at a Harvard Business School session focused on rediscovering leadership values—a shared moment of reflection, recalibration, and growth. The lesson? Even the most experienced leaders need intentional pauses to reflect and realign.

The same is true for you.

When your mental or emotional fuel tank feels low, that's your body's signal: it's time to refuel. Just as a car can't function without energy, neither can a leader. Many leaders who begin their journeys as great coaches slow down—not from lack of ability, but because they stop making themselves a priority.

Leadership doesn't ask less of you over time; it asks more. It's a gift that keeps on giving, which is exactly why we must commit to growing ourselves, coaching ourselves, and replenishing our energy so we can give from a place of wholeness, not depletion.

Your team isn't expecting you to have all the answers. But they are counting on your energy, your presence, and your belief to help fuel their own.

To sustain this, it's important to recognize the difference between short-term actions and long-term strategies. Many leaders struggle with balancing both ends of this spectrum—either over-indexing on quick fixes or deferring everything to the future.

Our good friend and executive coach Dorie Clark reminds us in her book *The Long Game* (Harvard Business Review Press, 2021) that visionary leadership requires intention, patience, and a commitment to sustained growth. She challenges leaders to resist short-term pressure and invest in long-term impact.

In the short term, start by activating your leadership accountability network. Reach out to trusted partners—colleagues, peers, or direct reports—and ask for support. Be open about where you need help. If you're not ready to share challenges with your leadership team, seek out internal allies or external mentors who can offer guidance.

For the long game, this is the moment to connect with a licensed coach or trusted advisor. Invest in your self-education—whether through tools, frameworks, or academic leadership programs—that can guide you through low seasons and help you lead from a place of steadiness, not strain.

Ultimately, it's up to the leader to choose the path back to strength. But here's the truth: leaders rarely have the luxury of delayed response. Effective leadership demands *proactive* action, not reactive coping. Leadership is visible—what you model, how you move, and the way you choose to care for yourself sets the tone for your team.

So choose wisely. How you nurture yourself back into strength is a powerful act of coaching prowess. You are both the MVP—and the trusted advisor—of yourself.

The Power of Coaching: A Tale of Three Leaders

Leadership isn't a solo journey. While strong habits of self-management are essential, the most effective leaders know when to bring in expert support—often before energy runs low or challenges become overwhelming. In earlier chapters and sections, we explored how self-leadership shapes success; now, we look at how personal coaching can deepen that foundation when more is needed.

Great leaders come to coaching prepared with their own tools and insights. Coaching doesn't replace self-leadership; it enhances it. By partnering with an experienced coach, leaders gain fresh perspectives, receive accountability, and find a tailored path to grow. This kind of support helps unlock new potential, reignite purpose, and build resilience—not just for the leader but also for the entire team.

What follows are the stories of three leaders—Elena, Daniel, and Carol—who each turned to personal coaching during challenging seasons. Their journeys show how coaching can start gently and directionally, introduce focused practices, and ultimately inspire a long-term commitment to growth and renewal.

Elena's Story: Rebuilding Culture from the Inside Out

When Elena first met her coach, she was running on fumes. As executive director of a mid-size nonprofit, she had just navigated a painful funding cut that forced layoffs and program reductions. Her team—once energized by mission—was quiet, withdrawn, and losing faith. Elena wasn't far behind them.

Her coach didn't start with a plan. She started with presence.

Their early sessions were restorative—a quiet space for Elena to name what had been lost, both in her organization and in herself. They didn't dive into strategy. Instead, they walked through values. "What first called you to this work?" her coach asked. "And what part of that still whispers to you?"

Those conversations marked the kind beginning—a soft return to purpose.

Then came the drills.

At first, Elena resisted. Her coach introduced daily leadership reflection exercises:

- Write down one thing you avoided today and why.
- Name the emotion you saw most in your team this week and how you contributed to it.
- Hold one 15-minute listening meeting each day, with no agenda.

They weren't complicated, but they were consistent. And they were uncomfortable. Elena began to realize how much she had retreated, not just from her team, but from her own leadership. The coaching got more structured:

- Role-play tough conversations before they happened.
- Practice energizing language in weekly check-ins.
- Track which team behaviors mirrored her own energy—day by day.

And slowly, things began to shift.

By the third month, Elena wasn't just showing up—she was *leading* again. But this time, with different muscles. Coaching wasn't about quick fixes. It became a practice. She began reading again—books on team resilience, trauma-informed leadership, even revisiting her graduate school notes. She made space in her calendar every Friday to "learn something on purpose."

This was the long game of self-education—not to earn a credential, but to earn her team's trust again.

The intentional strategy worked, and they noticed.

Morale didn't skyrocket overnight, but the team became more vocal in meetings. A junior colleague initiated a new donor engagement idea. Elena wasn't fixing everything. She was learning in public and inviting others to do the same.

Daniel's Story: Rewiring Leadership One Sprint at a Time

Daniel was known for his innovation. As a vice president at a fast-paced tech firm, he'd led teams that launched cutting-edge products and disrupted markets. But after a high-profile product failure, his team's confidence slipped, along with their willingness to take risks. Daniel felt stuck, frustrated, and unsure how to inspire his people again.

His coach began not by giving answers but by listening carefully.

In their first conversations, Daniel was guarded, dismissive even. The coach's tone was patient, gently curious: "What stories are you telling yourself about this failure? What part of your leadership feels hardest right now?" These questions cracked open his defenses and opened a small space for reflection: the kind start.

Then the real work began.

The coach introduced drills designed to disrupt Daniel's avoidance patterns:

- Each week, Daniel journaled about moments he'd felt defensive and rewrote the story from a growth mindset perspective.
- He practiced delivering candid feedback to team members during role-play sessions with the coach.
- He tracked daily decisions when he had the chance to empower others but hesitated.

At first, Daniel bristled against these exercises. But he realized they weren't criticisms; they were a mirror, showing how his habits were slowing the team's recovery.

Little by little, Daniel rewired his leadership behaviors. He stopped micromanaging product teams, invited more input, and modeled vulnerability by openly sharing what he was learning from the failure.

Coaching didn't stop when the sessions ended.

Daniel committed to the long game: signing up for leadership workshops, reading widely on emotional intelligence and agile management, and setting quarterly learning goals for himself and his team.

This intentional self-education rekindled his own confidence and, importantly, showed his team that setbacks were part of the journey, not a signal to give up.

Carol's Story: Finding Renewal Through Better Questions

Carol, a seasoned health care administrator, was facing a crisis. Staff turnover was at an all-time high, and the pressure of constant operational challenges left her exhausted and doubting her ability to lead effectively. The weight of burnout was heavy, not just on her team but on herself.

Her coach didn't rush to fix the problems.

Their early sessions were about kindness and curiosity—creating a safe space where Carol could honestly name her frustrations and fears without judgment. The coach asked questions like "What's the story you tell yourself about your leadership right now?" and "What small wins might you have overlooked?"

This slow, gentle approach helped Carol reconnect with her own leadership values and break through feelings of isolation.

Then came the coaching drills: a series of reflective and active exercises designed to build new habits:

- Tracking moments when she felt reactive and pausing before responding

- Practicing appreciative inquiry in team meetings to shift conversations toward strengths and possibilities
- Keeping a leadership journal to identify recurring patterns and blind spots

These practices felt awkward at first, but gradually gave Carol tools to manage stress and lead with more presence.

Most important, coaching reframed Carol's approach from seeking quick fixes to embracing the long game of learning.

She committed to continuous education: attending leadership seminars, studying organizational psychology, and mentoring emerging leaders. Coaching became a launchpad for a lifelong journey of growth, one question and one insight at a time.

Her renewed curiosity and intentional learning slowly restored the trust and commitment of her team, and gave Carol back her sense of purpose.

The stories of these three leaders highlight the kinds of challenges many leaders face in the workplace. No matter the situation, it remains our responsibility to confront those challenges—and to lead forward—with the support of self-leadership and trusted coaching.

Leading and Coaching from a Place of Strength

Leadership is a gift. When we become leaders, we often aspire to be seen as guiding others from a place of strength. But the reality of leadership comes with its inherent challenges—moments of both high impact and deep strain.

Leading from a place of strength doesn't mean having all the answers. It means showing up with clarity, emotional steadiness, and a willingness to grow—especially when circumstances are uncertain.

Effective leaders understand that true coaching prowess begins with managing themselves well. They recognize that their influence depends not only on their actions but also on their ability to lead and coach with clarity, consistency, and care. The success of a leader lies in understanding the delicate balance between leading others and coaching themselves from that place of strength.

- What does that place of strength look like for you?
- How do you plan to stay grounded in it as you grow in your leadership and impact?
- What habits and best practices from great coaches will you adopt?
- When will you pause to seek the support of your accountability partners?
- And when will you know it's time to invite in the guidance of an experienced coach?

These questions—and others like them—help us establish a thoughtful balance between mindset and energy. They remind us that coaching isn't just for crisis moments; it's a vital, ongoing tool for sustaining growth, refining habits, and staying anchored through the highs and lows of leadership.

Start small: reflect, reach out, or ask for feedback. Your next leadership breakthrough may begin with one coaching question, and your willingness to answer it honestly.

Leadership as Legacy: Grow, Coach, Repeat

Every decision, habit, and conversation becomes part of the leadership legacy we leave behind. Grow. Coach. Repeat—with purpose and intention.

Everything we've explored in this book matters. The stories, reflections, and insights are not just lessons; they are real moments our peers and colleagues have faced. Some we've witnessed while coaching executives; others we've lived ourselves. And some are thoughtfully crafted scenarios—experiments rooted in the realities leaders encounter every day.

Leadership is an evolving journey, one where vulnerability, reflection, and coaching are not signs of weakness, but powerful indicators of strength.

Our discussion of coaching prowess is meant to remind you that delivering great leadership will sometimes require a new kind of strength. It means knowing when to pause, when to ask for support, and when to return to the basics: starting kind, practicing daily drills, and recommitting to the long game of self-education. These habits shape how we face each day, one moment at a time.

This is also your opportunity to mean something more to your team. To reset your presence in the organization. To become not just a leader but the kind of coach your team can trust, learn from, and grow with. It's a chance to build a legacy as a leader who wasn't afraid of vulnerability, who knew when to look inward, and who led by nurturing others from the inside out.

We might not have all grown up with great coaching models. We might not have been coached like athletes. But we now know that self-leadership is a practice with infinite possibilities. And if we are to lead innovative teams, we must commit to learning who we are today—and who we are still becoming.

We must resist the urge to rush and perform. Instead, we must direct our energy toward inclusive leadership and extend grace to ourselves and those we lead. We must prioritize growth over ego and make time to understand all the players on our team—what drives them, what restores them—because leadership is visible. And how we lead is how they will learn to lead others.

This reflection sets the stage for the final chapter, where we explore the abundance that comes from humanizing coaching. Today's workplace calls for a new kind of leader: one who is ready to coach, nurture, and lead with kindness, care, and intention. But for that kind of leadership to take root, we must learn how to humanize coaching and how to coach our teams with empathy, clarity, and purpose.

9

How Can Humanizing Coaching Inspire Change?

Starting Human

For all great coaches, one of their earliest and most essential discoveries is this: start human. Whether working with senior executives in boardrooms or gifted students in classrooms, the mindset is the same: coach the human.

What unites us all is our shared humanity. Human-centered design. For humans, by humans. If we accept that we are humans first—and everything else second—then we must ask ourselves these questions:

- What is your mindset when you work with people?
- How do you lead the humans on your team?
- Do you see yourself in them, or do you see something else?

When a leader leads from a place of unrelatable significance, people feel the distance. But when a leader leads from a human place, people feel the connection. And then, they remember how your leadership made them feel: calm, seen, safe, supported, or inspired.

Today's workplace demands a more human-centered approach to leadership, one that treats each person as worthy of dignity, understanding, and care.

Yes, we are different. Our identities, experiences, and stories are unique. But when we don't relate from a human foundation, we lose the chance to deepen connection, build trust, and earn confidence.

And once trust is lost, the climb becomes uphill.

Coaching, leading, and connecting must begin with recognizing the human in front of you. It's the heart of transformational leadership—where presence meets empathy and impact begins with understanding.

The Classroom and the Workplace

One of the best places to test your leadership approach—and assess whether it's truly human-centered—is in the classroom. The classroom is a melting pot of dreams, anxieties, goals, lived experiences, early successes, painful failures, indecisions, and new beginnings. It brings together students from all walks of life, each carrying a unique story.

The first office hours session often reveals more than just academic concerns. It's filled with quiet, vulnerable questions: Am I in the right place? Am I smart enough? Can I handle the rigor? Will I succeed here? Did I make the right choice? Some call it *imposter syndrome*—we call it being human.

Starting something new—whether it's returning to school, investing in yourself differently, or changing course—shakes your sense of certainty. Even if you've been in school before, *you* have changed. This time, everything feels different because *you* are different.

And so your students come to you—sometimes nervously, sometimes with hope—looking for affirmation. They may not know you yet, but they instinctively hope you will see them, believe in them, and reflect something steady and strong back to them.

In that moment—whether you're ready or not—you are responsible: responsible for how they begin to see themselves, for the confidence they start to rebuild, and for the story they carry forward—not just through school, but in life.

The same is true in the workplace.

The humans you lead—whether you inherited them or they're joining you for the first time—carry similar questions and quiet uncertainties. And you, as their leader, are responsible for offering reassurance. Many leaders hope for a team that arrives fully equipped and self-sufficient. But here's the truth: even the most talented individuals need to feel seen, supported, and safe.

Students in the classroom are often just as capable as professionals in the workplace. What sets them apart is the presence of a built-in safety net, and the belief that their professor might meet them with kindness. By contrast, some leaders hide their most human, compassionate side, believing it's a weakness rather than a strength.

So we must ask you these questions:

- Why are you hiding?
- What are you hiding?

The classroom and the workplace are not so different. Both are filled with humans who want to succeed, learn, grow, and be seen. But they don't want to be judged.

One of the most powerful lessons I've ever learned about leading humans came from the classroom.

When our friend and girls' leadership coach Julie Carrier gave her keynote at the Thinkers50 Gala, she shared a profound truth: leadership starts in the classroom.

So ask yourself these questions:

- Is your workplace a classroom—one designed to nurture, inspire, and produce the best and brightest?
- Can your team come to you with their doubts, without fear?

In the classroom, students rarely fall behind because they lack intelligence. They got in—they earned their seat. But what most shapes their experience isn't their intellect. It's your leadership.

We get it; some leaders don't feel equipped to lead this way. But here's the truth: leading humans doesn't require advanced degrees or decades of experience. It simply starts with the awareness that the human in front of you could be you.

Ask the greatest coaches of all time what makes coaching truly effective, and they'll say it's about being *relatable*. Yes, power dynamics exist in the workplace. And yes, some still fear that being approachable erodes authority. But that's an outdated myth, one that leads to fearful leadership, disconnected teams, and ultimately, burnout.

Why lead from a place of distance when the most effective leaders are visible?

Great athletes often say their coaches are present, relatable, and reachable, that they *feel* seen and valued. So why don't we adopt the same mindset in the workplace? What if we coached our teams with that same spirit of availability, belief, and care? The performance would follow.

In the classroom, we see this clearly: how we guide and coach students shapes not only how they show up in school but also how they lead and live after. The same is true in the workplace. How you lead now influences how they will lead when they're promoted, transferred, or moved to new roles.

Leadership is not about being perfect. It's about being *visible*. And visibility isn't about performance—it's about *transformation*.

When we lead with humanity, others learn to lead with humanity. When we lead with compassion, they learn compassion. When we lead with empathy, they learn empathy. When we lead with kindness, they carry it forward. When we lead with intentionality, they discover purpose.

The pessimist in you might ask, "How do I know they'll lead the way I do?" The honest answer is that you don't. But to be the coach your team remembers, the one whose influence ripples forward—you show up anyway. You model what great leadership looks like.

When you choose to lead with the purest form of humanity, they respond.

As the semester progresses, their questions quiet down, and the anxiety eases because your leadership has given them tools not just to succeed but also to manage life and confront uncertainty in their thinking.

Sometimes, smart leadership means knowing when to refer them to professional support. Other times, it's simply about being there: offering grounded, human support when they need it most.

A great coach knows which questions to ask to understand the full depth of someone's circumstances and identify the actions that best support their growth.

What's often surprising is that your best students are sometimes the ones who struggle the most at the start. But with the right leadership, they find their way back to who they've always been: more refined, more focused, more purposeful, and more confident.

The same is true for top talent in the workplace.

The expectations in the classroom mirror those in the workplace. Both are competitive spaces, filled with individuals striving for excellence. In both environments, talented people are seeking your approval, your validation, your coaching, and your leadership. They want to learn from you.

Both spaces are filled with those quietly vying for your attention—yearning for your time, your guidance, and your commitment to their growth.

So, be the kind of leader who helps lift your team from a sunken place to one that aligns with their energy and purpose. Our workplaces are filled with talented individuals walking around in their feelings, often with little support to reset the false narratives they've internalized.

Leadership prowess in action—and what great coaches do best—is knowing how to read the room, understand the person, and guide them toward the victory they've been quietly fighting for on the inside.

There's nothing to fear. Fear often creeps in when leaders think, "If I help them become the best version of themselves, they'll leave me—or leave the organization." And yes, that's possible.

But it's a truth that professors understand well—students have a set term in a program, and eventually, they graduate. Great coaches understand it, too—top players may leave for a better opportunity. Yet we teach, we coach, we lead anyway.

We lead with humanity because we think differently. We believe in the cycle: Grow. Coach. Repeat.

If someone leaves for greener pastures, that's okay. They leave carrying your leadership legacy with them. And that's a powerful place for any leader to stand—to say, "While they were here, we did great things together. And now that they've moved on, they will continue to succeed—because I helped equip them to do so."

That is the quiet strength of great leadership: your impact remains, whether they stay or go. And more often than not, people stay—when their values align with your leadership and when they feel seen, supported, and stretched.

Help Them Find Their Voice

There are levels to the practice of leadership. Even the smartest, most talented team members need individualized support to find their voice. Leadership isn't one-size-fits-all; it's a thoughtful, adaptive practice that meets people where they are and helps bring out the power within.

When coach Patrick Mouratoglou began working with Serena Williams, one of the first things he noticed was that she didn't want to be told what to do. To some leaders, that kind of resistance might seem stubborn or closed-minded. Many might disengage or end the relationship through termination, reassignment, or withdrawal.

But Patrick approached it differently. As a mental coach, his instinct was to understand why. What if the talent isn't asking to be told what to do, but instead, is asking to be trusted, challenged, or empowered to lead themselves?

It's a reminder of the timeless principle: Give a person a fish, and they eat for a day. Teach them how to fish, and they eat for a lifetime.

Great leaders don't control voices; they help unlock them.

They invest the necessary time to understand what the talent is trying to teach them—about who they are, what they stand for, what drives them, how they respond to leadership, and how they react to your style.

Identifying their voice is essential. At global management consulting firm McKinsey & Company, much of their talent development strategy is proactive, centered on understanding what each individual wants to do next and the skills they'll need to get there.

When working with talent to help them discover their voice, one effective approach is to ask, What does finding your voice mean to you? Why do you feel disconnected from it? These questions uncover internal barriers and self-perceptions that may be holding them back.

The irony of growth is that as talent rises to higher levels in their careers, their voice often evolves. The more that's required of them, the more they may begin to question it. They start to worry about how they're perceived—about executive presence, authority, and composure. And sometimes, in the pursuit of "looking the part," they begin to lose touch with their authentic voice.

The same dynamic shows up in the classroom. When top students from across the globe gather in one space, even the most confident among them can begin to question themselves. The classroom becomes a live stage, a place where reactions are compared, intellect is silently measured, and validation is often sought through performance rather than presence.

In these moments, students can begin to shrink their voice—not because they lack brilliance, but because they're recalibrating in real time. They start to wonder how much of themselves is safe to reveal, what qualifies as "enough," and how they measure up against equally accomplished peers.

A student once shared that she felt inadequate because she wasn't as quick to respond to questions in class. Compared to her peers, their answers came faster—so she grew quieter, withdrawing not out of disinterest but out of quiet self-doubt.

The same thing happens in the workplace. When a leader expects rapid responses, even in casual brainstorming sessions, it can unintentionally slow down the rest of the team. It can make others feel insecure, especially if the unspoken message becomes "Your voice only matters if it's fast, sharp, and immediate."

This isn't to say competition is a bad thing. Healthy, respectful tension among talented people can be motivating. But like anything else in life, it requires balance. Without psychological safety, even high-performing individuals can begin to doubt themselves, holding back rather than leaning in.

That's why it's essential for leaders—whether in academic or professional spaces—to create environments where individuality is celebrated and voice isn't something to be earned but something to be owned.

Supporting your talent starts with giving them the stage and the space to participate and rehearse—without judgment. Create an environment where the expectation of excellence doesn't need to be spoken, because the intention is clear and the vision for success is evident.

Ultimately, the point is this: make time to truly know your team. Not in a rushed, dismissive way. Not as a task to check off a list. Not in a way that interrupts productivity or feels like babysitting.

But in the way great coaches do: by observing, listening, understanding conditions, noticing personality, responding in real time, and measuring what matters.

Helping your team discover their voice often requires going deeper. Be the leader who creates time. Be the leader who takes responsibility for making space. Be the leader who sees not just the talent in front of you but also the innovation and possibility within them. Be the leader who's not afraid to invest fully, even if they one day choose to walk away.

Teach Them What You Know

Marshall is known for saying, "Teach people everything you know." Why? Because we believe in the power of a learning mindset: the ability not only to absorb knowledge, but to transform mindsets and behaviors through it.

My mother, Chief Temitope Ajayi, HRH, often told us growing up, "Learn from the masters." To her, the master symbolized the importance of learning directly from the source: from those who have achieved success and are willing to help others become even better versions of themselves.

In my classroom, that philosophy guides my mission. I aim to teach my students everything I know—not just academic frameworks and principles but also real-world lessons about life, career, and leadership.

The goal isn't for them to become like me. It's to enrich their journey with the benefit of my experiences, insights, and knowledge so they can define success on their own terms.

The classroom is often the easiest place to do this. The learning objectives are clear: learn, reflect, adapt, and be transformed. But the workplace can be just as powerful, especially under leaders who are willing to share what they know. When that happens, teams don't just perform better—they evolve.

TJ, a chief operating officer at an engineering firm, became known for creating champions. Many of his direct reports rose through the ranks, and word quickly spread about his success. Soon, everyone wanted to be on his team—just like athletes who are eager to switch teams when there's a great coach at the helm.

TJ's leadership philosophy was simple: teach what I know, and then watch them blossom as they adapt those lessons to their own path. He knew that confidence grows when people feel they're learning from someone who's walked the road before them.

I once invited a close colleague—let's call him Paul—to be a guest speaker in my course. When he declined immediately, I was shocked. Most of my guest speaker invitations are met with enthusiasm—speakers are typically eager to engage with students. So when he responded with a firm no, I asked why.

His answer: "I don't want to teach anyone what I know."

I was stunned. This was someone who held a senior leadership role at a major advertising firm. Quietly, I began to wonder what his team thought of him and his leadership style. I didn't try to convince him otherwise, because I, too, am protective of the kinds of leaders I expose to my brilliant students.

Anyone who responds that way to an invitation to share knowledge with the next generation may not be the right fit for that kind of audience—not because they lack expertise, but because they're not ready to lead with generosity.

Be generous with what you know, even in highly competitive workplaces where fear of being replaced often looms. Yes, these situations can happen. But if an organization chooses to demote you and promote someone you mentored, that says more about the organization's values than your decision to lead with generosity.

The truth is, secure leaders share what they've learned. They're not threatened by rising talent—they're fueled by it. Encouraged by it. Eager to support. Ready to serve. They understand that legacy isn't defined by what they hold on to, but by what they generously pour into others.

Teaching others what you know doesn't diminish your value; it multiplies your impact. You become a force multiplier. A builder of people. A shaper of futures. An architect of coaching prowess. A leadership entrepreneur.

When you teach from a place of abundance, you're not just transferring skills—you're passing along belief, confidence, and clarity.

Great leaders know that knowledge hoarded becomes stagnant. But knowledge shared? That becomes power in motion—an investment that keeps growing.

They pass them on. Your wisdom echoes forward. Your coaching becomes a defining experience—remembered as the moment someone gained direction, clarity, and a renewed sense of purpose.

So teach them what you know—not for recognition, but so they can rise. Because that's what true leadership does: it lifts others higher.

Show Them You're Truly Invested

My friend and global storyteller Anita Erskine once shared in an interview with Manal Bernoussi: "Leadership is not a title. It's an experience. And it's an experience shaped by people who believe that in your hands, they can entrust their lives, their dreams, and their ambitions."

Her words offer a powerful reminder that intentional leadership is not about position—it's about how our team experiences us. It's about the trust they place in us and the investment we're willing to make in their growth and future.

These same actions and expectations are mirrored in the classroom.

So pause and ask yourself these questions:

- When was the last time you told your team that you're just as invested in them as they are in themselves?
- When was the last time your leaders said the same to you?
- How would it make you feel to hear those words?
- And how might your team respond if you said them aloud?

Leaders come in all shapes and sizes, and their core beliefs endure—expressed through their actions and how they lead. We don't blame anyone for not responding perfectly to this kind of leadership. Instead, the goal is to shift your mindset toward one that recognizes leading humans requires humanistic tactics and genuine connection.

Making your team feel that you are just as invested in their success is essential—an unignorable and nonnegotiable circumstance in effective leadership.

In the classroom, students can immediately sense whether a professor is truly invested in them. It's reflected in their actions:

the way they lead discussions, the experiences they choose to share, and their teaching style.

The same is true in leadership. How we express our level of investment in talent is obvious because leadership is visible. Much of what we do as leaders isn't hidden; it's seen, felt, and experienced.

Leadership is love made visible. And investing in others is a form of love. It requires effort. It takes intention. But it's always worthwhile.

Investment fuels innovation, fosters creativity, builds commitment, and earns trust. At its core, investment creates a culture of giving and receiving, one that empowers people to show up fully and grow forward.

The Other Side of Leadership

We live in a world where everyone brings their past experiences—both good and painful—into the workplace. Some call it trauma when it's difficult to process. Others call it a tacit experience when it shapes us quietly and constructively.

The challenge for leaders is learning to adjust their coaching and leadership style to individuals who may not be ready—or willing—to release themselves from past pain. As a result, they may not respond favorably to your guidance, even when it's well-intentioned.

So what do you do then?

As much as we want leaders to consistently show up with presence, clarity, and prowess, we must also acknowledge that some people carry hurt and disappointment that distorts how they experience even the kindest form of leadership.

How can leaders navigate scenarios like this?

You pause. You assess. You recalibrate. You create a coaching response tailored to that individual, one that gently explores whether their resistance is rooted in your leadership approach, a deeper challenge with authority, unresolved organizational trauma, personal disappointment in their own growth, or even a lack of job satisfaction.

The point here is this: even the best leaders—those capable of coaching high-performing teams—will sometimes encounter talent who simply doesn't respond to their guidance. In those moments, it's critical to maintain your humanity. Lead with compassion and empathy, while also protecting your own sense of leadership. Don't let one negative response distort your belief in your ability or cloud how others are experiencing your leadership.

Sometimes, that individual may just need more time with you—this could be their way of asking for your attention. Other times, they may be silently struggling with personal challenges, unaware that their inner battles are showing up in their work and affecting the workplace around them.

This is where emotional intelligence becomes the gift that keeps on giving, especially for a leader whose actions are being closely observed and admired by others.

Jose was a senior executive at a consulting firm. When his team expanded, two new team members were added under his leadership. Right away, Jose relied on his coaching prowess to bring them up to speed: introducing them to the team's culture, expectations, and dynamics.

Up until that point, Jose was well liked by his team. Everyone responded favorably to his leadership, and his reputation across the organization was strong.

But what wasn't immediately obvious was the context behind the new additions. Their previous leader had been laid off, and their former team was dissolved. The two talents had been reassigned and, in many ways, felt like children navigating the emotional terrain of a recent divorce—displaced and still emotionally tethered to their former manager.

Because of their loyalty to their previous leader, they struggled to embrace Jose's leadership and adapt to the new team culture. And despite his best efforts, Jose found himself facing quiet resistance.

Rather than taking it personally, Jose drew from his coaching mindset and leaned into a different approach: one grounded in our principles of humanized leadership. This is the very question we explore in this chapter: can humanizing coaching inspire change? Jose's story shows us that it can. What follows in his actions isn't a formula; it's a human-centered approach to coaching, built on small but powerful shifts that inspire connection, trust, and growth.

We've organized these principles into four key steps, introduced earlier in the chapter. The following summary demonstrates how you—just like Jose—can apply these humanized leadership strategies in moments that challenge or stretch your coaching prowess.

Step 1: Start Human

Leadership begins with presence, not performance. Jose didn't immediately rush to assert authority—he paused to see the two people in front of him. He recognized that resistance is often rooted in emotion, not defiance. So he led with empathy, not ego.

Instead of taking it personally, Jose chose to pause, assess, and recalibrate—a hallmark of emotional intelligence. He recognized that the resistance he was facing might not be about his leadership ability at all, but rather about their emotional response to sudden change and the disruption of losing a trusted leader. With over 19 years of experience in leadership and management, Jose was no stranger to navigating different personalities and complex team dynamics.

Step 2: Show Them You're Truly Invested

Jose took time to meet with each of them individually—not to talk to them, but to listen. He didn't rush to assert his authority or demand buy-in. Instead, he made it clear: "I'm just as invested in your success as you are." He asked about their aspirations, how they were adjusting, and what they missed most about their former team.

This act of intentional presence shifted the dynamic. To their surprise, they felt seen, not managed. Jose's willingness to understand their story, rather than control it, created a bridge. Over time, they also began to recognize and respect his leadership identity and receptiveness to their new teammates.

Step 3: Teach Them What You Know

Jose began sharing more of his leadership journey—not through directives, but through stories. He spoke about how he had navigated change in his own career, how he built trust with his teams, and how he created space for others to grow. His goal wasn't to be admired; it was to help them rise. He even recommended books on organizational management and workplace culture, encouraging them to think like leaders and grow into the potential he already saw in them.

By demystifying his own process and inviting them into it, he opened a door to mutual respect. It wasn't about erasing what they had before—it was about adding value to who they were becoming now and how they were adapting to new leadership and a new team.

Step 4: Help Them Find Their Voice

As trust began to grow, Jose encouraged them to lead small initiatives and present new ideas. He celebrated their contributions in team meetings and gave them room to speak without interruption. Over time, they began to show up differently: more confident, more connected, and more willing to collaborate.

Jose's success wasn't just in integrating them into the team; it was in helping them find their place and their voice again. The experience gave them a new sense of confidence, one that felt distinct from their past team dynamics.

We share this story to equip you with more tools for stretching your coaching prowess, especially when things don't go as planned or when the situation feels flipped from what you expected.

To effectively demonstrate coaching prowess, leaders must remain mindful of the many dynamics at play in today's workplace. Every team member brings their own history, mindset, and emotional landscape to the job. Great leaders don't just coach; they adapt, listen, and lead with intention. They understand that leadership is not a fixed style but a flexible practice shaped by the needs of those they serve.

Always take bold action as a leader—action that reflects your uniqueness, inspires change, and encourages thoughtfulness, innovation, and courageous effort in those you lead.

In the end, we ask you this question: are you willing to lead with the kind of presence, patience, and purpose that great coaching requires? Coaching prowess isn't about having all the answers; it's about showing up fully for the people you lead. When you lead with humanity, listen with empathy, teach with generosity, and invest with intention, you do more than manage a team—you transform lives.

And that is the kind of leadership that lasts—inspirational, remembered, and carried forward.

Final Thoughts:
The Reader's Challenge

Congratulations—you've reached the final chapter of this book.

This section was written just for you—to mark this moment and celebrate your commitment to learning and leading with purpose. It is our way of saying that we see you. We honor your courage to lead a life that not only uplifts others but also renews your own spirit and the leadership excellence you aspire to achieve.

Scientia potentia est—as you may recall from Chapter 3—means knowledge is power. Not just in theory, but in how we choose to use it. When applied with intention, learning becomes more than information. It becomes a transformation.

Throughout this book, you've been invited to embrace a leadership mindset rooted in curiosity, intentionality, and growth—for yourself and for others. This is what we call *leadership prowess*: the bold choice to lead through learning, to coach with humanity, and to grow with purpose.

It's not about perfection—but presence.

Not about control—but contribution.

Not about fear—but generosity.

If you're reading these words, it means something important: you've either completed the journey or you were drawn here early by a deeper desire to grow into the kind of leader this world needs.

Either way, you're here. And that means you're ready.

Ready to commit to the reader's challenge.

At the end of each day, take a quiet moment to reflect and ask yourself these questions:

Was I willing today?

Was I intentional today?

Did I nurture someone's potential today?

Write down one moment—big or small—where your leadership reflects the WIN mindset. Let this be your daily check-in. Let this be your legacy in motion.

Because when you choose to WIN, you inspire others to do the same.

Our friend and chief learning officer, Dr. Ruth Gotian, shared four tips for retaining learning in an *NBC News* interview: write what you learned in your own words, reflect before applying new ideas, experiment by applying new ideas immediately, and leverage technology to keep records.

As you begin to apply the strategies, insights, and frameworks shared throughout this book, remember to pass that knowledge on. Share it with your team or your leadership accountability circle. Because knowledge becomes more powerful and even more purposeful when it's shared—and it opens doors to new possibilities not just for you but also for those you lead and those around you.

Whether you're deciding on the kind of leadership legacy you want to leave or reflecting on new habits you're ready to build into your leadership life, our hope is that this book has stretched your mindset and challenged your thinking.

When you re-enter the world—your workplace, your classroom, your community—know that something within you has shifted. And others will see it.

Because leadership is visible.

Your leadership is visible.

It reflects your values. It shapes your culture. It inspires those around you.

And when you lead with our WIN mindset of willingness, intentionality, and nurturing, you take leadership to a higher level. A level grounded in mutual respect, trust, and empathy.

When you choose to WIN, you inspire others to do the same.

Not just through actions but through intentional, decisive leadership that welcomes experimentation, embraces vulnerability, and prioritizes mindfulness:

Leadership that begins with kindness
Leadership that practices new habits daily
Leadership that grows you into the coach your team deserves

Remember this always: leadership is an experience—one shaped by courageous actions, kindness at the forefront, patience with the process, a passion for coaching others, and a lifelong commitment to learning.

Inspired by the spirit of this book, remember that leadership is not a final destination but a lifelong journey—one that invites us to grow, to serve, and to uplift others along the way. The true measure of leadership is the positive change we inspire in the lives we touch.

It is never too late to start, and never too early to adjust.

In the words of Mahatma Gandhi, "Be the change you wish to see in the world."

We expand on this profound wisdom from a prolific coach the world has come to know, "Be the leader you want to see more of in the world."

Together, these truths invite you to lead with intention, to serve with heart, and to transform the world one courageous step at a time.

Take a moment now to envision the leader you aspire to be. What small step can you take today to live into that vision?

Remember, leadership is a shared journey. Reach out, connect, and grow alongside those around you and within your leadership accountability circle.

Together, we can cultivate cultures of courage, kindness, and continuous learning.

With courage and heart, the future of leadership is yours to shape.

We leave you with the powerful words of Dr. Brené Brown: "dare to lead."

Further Reading

Bregman, Peter. *Leading with Emotional Courage: How to Have Hard Conversations, Create Accountability, and Inspire Action on Your Most Important Work*. Wiley, 2018.

Brown, Brené. *Dare to Lead: Brave Work. Tough Conversations*. Whole Hearts, 2018.

Cohn, Alisa. *From Start-Up to Grown-Up: Grow Your Leadership to Grow Your Business*. Kogan Page, 2021.

DeLong, Thomas J. *Flying Without a Net: Turn Fear of Change into Fuel for Success*. Harvard Business Review Press, 2011.

Goldsmith, Marshall, and Mark Reiter. *Triggers: Creating Behavior That Lasts–Becoming the Person You Want to Be*. Currency, 2015a.

Goldsmith, Marshall, and Mark Reiter. *What Got You Here Won't Get You There: How Successful People Become Even More Successful!* Hachette Books, 2015b.

Goldsmith, Marshall, and Mark Reiter. *The Earned Life. Lose Regret. Choose Fulfillment*. Crown Currency, 2022.

Harvard Business Review Press. *HBR At 100: The Most Influential and Innovative Articles from the Harvard Business Review's First Century*. Harvard Business Review Press, 2022.

Helgesen, Sally. *How We Can Bridge Divides and Create a More Inclusive Workplace*. Hachette Go Books, 2023.

Hesselbein, Francess, Marshall Goldsmith, and Sarah McArthur. *Work Is Love Made Visible: A Collection of Essays about the Power of Finding Your Purpose from the World's Greatest Thought Leaders*. Wiley, 2018.

Keating, Keith. *The Trusted Learning Advisor: The Tools, Techniques and Skills You Need to Make L&D a Business Priority*. Kogan Page, 2023.

Keating, Keith. *Hidden Value: How to Reveal the Impact of Organizational Learning*. Jetlaunch, 2025.

Melnick, Sharon. *In Your Power: React Less, Regain Control, Raise Others*. Wiley, 2022.

Mouratoglou, Patrick. *Champion Mindset: Coach Yourself to Win at Life*. Workman Publishing, 2025.

Nyamayaro, Elizabeth. *Human Skills: The Power to Connect with Anyone & Navigate Workplace Differences.* Prose, 2025.

Obama, Michelle. *The Light We Carry: Overcoming in Uncertain Times.* Crown Publishing, 2022.

Osman, Scott, Jacquelyn Lane, and Marshall Goldsmith. *Becoming Coachable. Unleashing the Power of Executive Coaching to Transform Your Leadership and Life.* 100 Coaches Publishing, 2023.

Paine, Nigel. *Workplace Learning: How to Build a Culture of Continuous Employment Development,* 2nd ed. Kogan Page, 2021.

Ricchiuto, Jack. *The Mindful Leader.* 2024.

Rometty, Ginni. *Good Power: Leading Positive Change in Our Lives, Work, and World.* Harvard Business Review Press, 2023.

Siang, Sanyin. *The Launch Book: 50 Ways to Launch Your Idea, Business or Next Career.* LID Publishing, 2017.

tha God, Charlamagne. *Shook One: Anxiety Playing Tricks on Me.* Atria Books, 2018.

Webb, Caroline. *How to Have a Good Day: Harness the Power of Behavioral Science to transform Your Working Life.* Currency, 2016.

Acknowledgments

Dr. Lilian Ajayi Ore

I want to express my deepest gratitude to my husband and two children. Your faith in me has been my greatest superpower, and your love remains a daily source of strength and inspiration. Thank you for being my unwavering support system—and my greatest pillar of accountability.

To my mother—my first and truest example of leadership—thank you for nurturing the unseen talents in me and my siblings. Your sacrifices and steadfast belief in us have shaped the woman I am today.

To my extended family and close friends—your continued support of me and my endeavors is a gift I hold close to my heart.

To my professional networks on LinkedIn and my university colleagues—your encouragement continues to inspire me to grow, question, and lead with purpose.

To my brilliant coauthor, Marshall Goldsmith—thank you for your wisdom, generosity, humanity, and never-ending belief in the power of collaborative leadership. It has been an honor and a true privilege to partner with you on this journey.

To the Marshall Goldsmith 100 Coaches community—thank you for being my champions and for reminding me of the power of shared purpose and collective wisdom. A very special thank you to Eric Schurenberg for your thoughtful Foreword and for being a strong and committed supporter of this book.

To my Global Connections for Women Foundation community—thank you for the lessons on purposeful leadership and for walking alongside me on this journey.

To my publishing team at Wiley—thank you for your professionalism and support. A special thank you to Kelly Talbot for being an exceptional writing coach, editor, and friend.

To all my students—past, present, and future—thank you for being a constant source of inspiration and for reminding me why the journey of learning and teaching never truly ends.

And finally, to you, our readers—thank you for your trust and belief in this work.

Dr. Marshall Goldsmith

There are several individuals and communities to whom I owe a heartfelt debt of gratitude—those who have significantly shaped my journey, my thinking, and my purpose.

First and foremost, I honor my mentors—Peter Drucker, Frances Hesselbein, Warren Bennis, Ken Blanchard, Paul Hersey, and Allan Mulally—each of whom profoundly influenced my career and leadership philosophy. Their wisdom, generosity, and example continue to guide not only my work but also how I strive to show up in the world.

I also want to acknowledge the extraordinary 100 Coaches community—a powerful network rooted in generosity, collaboration, and shared learning. This group embodies the very essence of servant leadership, and I am proud to walk alongside such purpose-driven individuals who lift others up with intention and care.

To my family and friends, thank you for your unwavering support, patience, and encouragement. Your love has been my foundation through every chapter of this journey, and I am deeply grateful for your presence in my life.

To my clients and readers around the world—thank you. Your trust in my work, and your commitment to becoming better leaders, better colleagues, and better people, has been the greatest reward of all. Your growth and success are the living legacy of the ideas I've had the privilege to share.

Finally, I want to express my deep appreciation to my coauthor, Dr. Lilian Ajayi Ore. Collaborating with you on this book has been an inspiring journey. Your vision, discipline, and powerful belief in the power of learning have brought fresh perspective and purpose to every page. I look forward to seeing how your voice continues to shape the future of leadership.

About the Authors

Dr. Lilian Ajayi Ore is the founder and CEO of Global Connections for Women Foundation and part of the Lead Faculty at Columbia University School of Professional Studies. She holds a EdD from the University of Pennsylvania's Graduate School of Education and has more than 17 years of industry experience. Her professional background spans leadership roles at Fortune 100 and 500 companies, where she developed deep expertise in learning, marketing, research, and digital innovation. She has also designed and led various academic and executive programs—including graduate and doctoral-level courses, entrepreneurship initiatives, faculty development workshops, and global corporate partnerships—affecting learners and executives across sectors and continents. A member of Marshall Goldsmith's 100 Executive Coaches, Lilian has been featured in *Forbes*, Harvard Business Publishing Education, Inc Magazine and Fast Company, and Entrepreneur.com and has provided keynote addresses in over 50 cities. Lilian is a recipient of several prestigious awards and recognition including Top 50 Learning and Development Professional, Top 100 Women list, Inspiring Voice in Academia by Harvard Business Impact, and President's Gold Volunteer Service award.

Dr. Marshall Goldsmith is a member of the *Thinkers50* Hall of Fame and the only two-time, number one Leadership Thinker in the world. He has been ranked the number one Executive Coach in the world for many years. Marshall is a number one *The New York Times*–bestselling author, and his books have sold over four million copies and have been published in 36 languages. His *The New York Times* bestsellers are *What Got You Here Won't Get You There*, *MOJO*, *Triggers*, and *The Earned Life*. Dr. Goldsmith's clients have included over 200 major CEOs and multiple leaders who have been recognized as CEO of the Year in the United States. His current mission is to share all that he knows with as many people as he can around the world.

Index